The Accidental Sal

NETWORKING SURVI

C000284653

The Accidental Salesman®

NETWORKING
SURVIVAL GUIDE

RICHARD WHITE

bookshaker

First published in the United Kingdom 2011
by Bookshaker.com

© Copyright Richard White

All rights reserved. No part of this publication may be reproduced, stored in or introduced into a retrieval system, or transmitted, in any form, or by any means (electronic, mechanical, photocopying recording or otherwise) without the prior written permission of the publisher.

This book is sold subject to the condition that it shall not, by way of trade or otherwise, be lent, resold, hired out, or otherwise circulated without the publisher's prior consent in any form of binding or cover other than that in which it is published and without a similar condition including this condition being imposed on the subsequent purchaser.

PRAISE

"A practical and easy-to-read guide to winning more business by networking."
Mike Southon, Financial Times columnist and best-selling business author

"This book neatly bridges the gap between the many books on networking skills and the many books on selling skills. This book will show you firstly how to attract more opportunities when networking, and then move your prospects from 'I want to work with you' to 'when can we start?'"
Heather Townsend, Author of FT Guide to Business Networking

"This book is about generating more offline business through better understanding the value you bring to the market place and better communicating your message through your network. This is a key area of focus at the Ecademy Digital School. I believe this book provides a valuable resource to survive not only in the offline world but in the online world too."
Thomas Power, Chairman Ecademy.com

"At NRG we believe networking is about developing business through the power of advocacy. The Networking Survival Guide gives you practical help on how to craft stories of the value you provide to your clients. A simple but powerful technique in developing advocacy."
David Clarke, CEO NRG Networks

"If networking is an important part of your marketing strategy then this is a must read! The Networking Survival Guide is packed with advice and some useful exercises to perfect your skills."
Warren Cass, Chief Executive Business Scene

"Richard's APPEAL framework for developing focused and specific sales messages manages to effectively cover the key areas many businesses miss and takes the reader through a powerful process to enhance their networking."

Andy Lopata, business networking strategist and co-author of bestselling ...and Death Came Third! The Definitive Guide to Networking and Speaking in Public

"Packed with wisdom, core principles and accessible, practical tips to upskill even the keenest of non-networkers. Worthy of a place on anyone's bookshelf."

Rob Brown, Motivational Speaker and author of bestselling book, How to Build Your Reputation

"Richard's book is full of practical advice on how to increase your sales at little to no cost! His 'non sales' background will give great comfort to all those professionals who always feel a little uncomfortable trying to grow their business. Here is a blue print for communicating value without being seen as a pushy 'sales type!'"

Andrew Wood, Author of Cunningly Clever Selling and CEO of CunninglyClever.com

"It's hard to make a sale when you have no sales leads. Networking builds relationships and generates sales leads. This easy to read book shows you how to develop and nurture relationships that will lead to more sales. That's a big payoff!"

Dr. Tony Alessandra, author of Collaborative Selling and co-developer of The Cyrano CRM Marketing System

"The Networking Survival Guide has made an immediate impact on my ability to leverage executive relationships and influences within and outside of banking clients to meet my business objectives. The A.P.P.E.A.L. process has been of particular value to me in distilling my value proposition and my target audience."

Rob Peters, Senior Business Development Executive, Computer Sciences Corp

ACKNOWLEDGEMENTS

I would like, first of all, to thank my clients who have entrusted me with helping them quickly turn around their sales fortunes through networking. Each client is different and helps to polish the process and I love to hear their stories and help them discover their golden nuggets.

A big thank you to my many teachers in NLP and NLP Coaching over the last twenty years which have all had their impact on this subject area in some way – especially in the area of communication and influence, and modelling excellence. These include Richard Bandler, John Grinder, Robert Dilts, Tad James, Christina Hall, Wyatt Woodsmall, Sue Knight, Paul McKenna, Michael Breen, Ian McDermott, Ian Ross, and Lisa Turner.

A special thank you goes to Espen Holm whose mentoring has taken my storytelling skills to a whole new level. Another important mentor has been Thomas Power, Chairman of Ecademy.com who has mentored me over the years on networking mindset. He is a true networking visionary and continues to nudge me in the right direction!

I would like to thank Christine Clacey whose encouragement of my storytelling work led to my workshop "Storytelling for referrals" which subsequently became the "Lead Generation Master Class" on which the content of this book is based. Christine helped me get the workshop off the ground and provided valuable feedback.

My big Ecademy BlackStar network has been a great source of encouragement and input over the last six years and have been a rich source of referrals for my work. There are too many people to name but you know who you are!

In helping me get my book completed I thank Mindy Gibbins-Klein and Tom Evans for their coaching, training, and advice.

Finally, I would like to thank my wife, Caroline, for her patience and support and also being a role model in the art of telling anecdotes that people want to listen to. This has had a major influence on my style of storytelling for developing relationships and sales leads.

FOREWORD

In 1985, I started BNI®, the world's largest business referral organisation, with the initial purpose of marketing my own consulting business—it didn't even occur to me that BNI would someday become a business in itself. Cold calling, which was then the most common tactic for generating new business, wasn't getting me anywhere and I had a mortgage to pay. I knew immediately that building a network of relationships to generate a steady stream of word-of-mouth referrals was important to me as a consultant; I just didn't fully realise at that time how crucially important it was for *all* business people *everywhere.*

Now, over twenty five years later, networking has more than proven itself as a cost-effective form of marketing that really *works*, and word-of-mouth referrals are universally seen as a much better way to generate new business than cold calling. BNI now has hundreds of thousands of members across the globe that generate billions in business for each other each year, and I have spent my entire business career focusing on helping businesses and organisations, large and small, understand the power and potential of networking. Believe me when I say that networking truly is *powerful*!

Effective networking can take a business on the verge of closing its doors to a thriving, successful operation even in an uncertain economy. The idea of growing your business through word-of-mouth marketing is a concept that crosses cultural, ethnic, and political boundaries because we all speak the language of referrals, and we all want to do business based on trust.

If you haven't started actively networking for your business, the perfect time to start is now and the perfect place to start is by reading the *Networking Survival Guide*. Richard White is a master networker with an extensive business background and a passion for helping others achieve success. Whether you are new to networking or you've been networking for years, utilising Richard's unique, dynamic, results-oriented approach to networking will set you up for lasting business growth and success.

A how-to guide with practical exercises to help you refine your sales message and communicate your business to others when networking, the strategies outlined in this book are invaluable along the path to developing a stream of regular referrals. Even if you believe you already know the networking basics, this book will open your eyes to new ways to maximize the results you're getting from your networking efforts.

There are networking opportunities everywhere we turn and the *Networking Survival Guide* provides the blueprint for turning those opportunities into real business referrals. When you arm yourself with the networking knowledge set forth in these pages, you will learn to recognise and strategically leverage the opportunities presented to you; never again will you leave money sitting on the table.

Dr Ivan Misner
NY Times Bestselling Author and
Founder of BNI and Referral Institute

CONTENTS

INTRODUCTION

David was at his wits' end. A year ago he had given up a well paid job to run his own business as an IT consultant. He had been investing a lot of time in networking as he had heard that it was an excellent way to find clients. Yet after a year he had little to show for his efforts. His income was barely enough to cover the cost of attending events and an endless diet of cooked breakfasts and coffee was doing his waistline no favours. He was beginning to think that maybe he should give up on his dream and get a job.

One of my advocates introduced me as someone who could help David clarify his proposition and by the end of the following day he managed to generate two big sales-leads. The big surprise for David was that the sales-leads came via people he thought he knew very well.

Why had David's networking proven to be so unfruitful despite all his efforts? Why was it that people close to him had not come forward previously with these sales-leads? What did David do differently?

By the end of reading this book you will not only have the answers but you will also be able to apply the same process to your own networking; and if you are already getting results it will become even more productive.

Just imagine how different things would be if you had more business coming in than you could handle. Rather than you having to cold call, your prospects are calling you. You have little competition and most sales close without much effort on your part.

Does this sound like the way you would like to do business?

How would your life be impacted? What new options would you have to better provide for your family? Would you live where you currently live? Would you go on the same holidays? Would you shop at the same grocery store? How much more fun will you have?

What Do I Mean By Networking?

If you picked up this book because of the words "sales-leads" in the title and are unsure of what I mean by "networking" then I should, at this point, lay down some definitions.

Sales-leads are expressions of interest in your products and services. You will need to put in some additional effort to close the deal.

By networking, I am referring to business networking and not computer networking. If you are a computer networking specialist then you may find some common themes but there are no cables involved!

Wikipedia, the online encyclopaedia, defines business networking as:

> *A socioeconomic activity by which groups of like-minded business-people recognise, create, or act upon business opportunities. A business network is a type of social network whose reason for existing is business activity.*

Business networking provides so many additional benefits over and above the generation of sales-leads. A good business network can provide things like support, friendship and advice. Some of my closest friends have come into my life as a direct result of business networking. In times of crisis people in my network are the first people I turn to. They keep me grounded and hold me to account. However, in this book I am specifically referring to networking as the activities we engage in to meet people and build our social network for the purpose of generating sales-leads.

I like to think of networking as "net" working. We build up a network of useful connections and resources and at the same time we build a net in which to land sales-leads in the same way some people use a net for fishing.

Despite all the intangible and unexpected benefits of a network, I believe there is one underlying motivation for most people who get up far too early in the morning or miss valuable family time in order to meet other business people; to generate a stream of sales-leads. Some engage in networking to supplement other marketing activities and cold calling. For others it is their only method of generating sales-leads. No matter how networking fits within your business marketing strategy I feel I am safe to assume that the very fact that you are reading this book means that you want to make the time you devote to networking more productive in terms of generating real business.

This is not a book for complete beginners. I will not be taking time to "sell" the idea of networking. I am assuming that you have already been "sold" on the promise that, when it works, it provides a rich source of opportunities that have less competition and are far easier to close than cold calling. I meet so many sales people who have given networking a try and, after a period of great enthusiasm, write it off as a waste of time. I also meet other non-sales people who run their own business and attend lots of meetings with precious little to show for their time and effort. This book will reveal what I have found to be the essential ingredients to make networking work.

A Process Is Born

This book is not theory. It is based on research that I have collected and tested over the last ten years. My research has included trial and error, being mentored by some prolific and successful business networkers and, most importantly for you, working with clients to help them generate more sales-leads from networking. The results I have gained from working with clients is what has given me the confidence to write this book.

David's story at the beginning of the chapter is a true story but I have changed the name. I had been working with lots of people helping them to improve their sales messaging and developing better propositions. I had also been teaching the use of storytelling in sales. It was when I worked with David one cold dark evening in a hotel lobby in Guildford that all the various strands converged. I have to admit that I was shocked at how fast we got results. I had achieved great results with clients but normally it was weeks or months. This was less than twenty four hours!

To create a repeatable process that could be taught to others, I retraced the steps David and I went through. I worked with a number of people and got similar results. From nothing to sales-leads in a matter of days. In some cases they were with people my clients had never met before. One client generated several sales-leads a couple of days later when networking at an exhibition. Since then, either on a one-on-one basis or at public master classes, I have helped many hundreds of people improve the productivity of their networking through the use of the same process.

I ran my first public Lead Generation Master Class in March 2006. I devised a one-day workshop which enabled me to take a large group of people through the process at the same time using a style of group training called *networkshops* that I pioneered back in early 2004. They are designed to help people improve their skills but also to network too. Over forty people attended my first master class, and I am delighted to say we had large numbers of people leave with sales-leads from other attendees. For some it was the first ever time that they had received sales-leads from networking.

The process works. It is simple and repeatable. This book will take you through the same process that was successful for David and hundreds of other networkers. I have included extra useful background information to help put the process into context and provide the right mindset for the process to work for you.

How To Get The Most From This Book

In this book I answer these regularly asked questions:

- How can I better explain what I do?
- How can I make my products and services sound more APPEALing to potential clients?
- How can I make my networking more productive?

By working through this book and applying it to your own situation, each of those questions will be answered. My desire is that by the time you have completed this book you will be able to generate more sales-leads, both from new contacts you make on your travels and from your existing contacts.

I am a great fan of books you can just 'dip in and out' of and you can do that with this book up to a certain point, although I recommend that you read through the book first before doing the exercises. There is a lot to help you better understand how to network more effectively and productively, but the real power of the process will only come once you have applied it to your sales messages by completing the exercises.

I look forward to guiding you through this journey, and wish you every success.

Best wishes

Richard White

one

SMALL DIFFERENCES CAN MAKE A BIG DIFFERENCE

I can remember when I first met David. It was at a networking lunch event in London. We were seated at the same table and I remember him being a warm, very friendly person. Tall and quite thin with a mop of curly black hair. He looked very professional in his dark blue suit. He was quite confident until it came to the point where we had to introduce ourselves to the rest of the table. His confidence seemed to evaporate and he started to look slightly uncomfortable.

David told us that he was an IT consultant and then spent a couple of minutes explaining the technology he worked with. As I looked at the faces around the table I could see nothing but glazed eyes! People were smiling and being polite and I am pretty sure that I was not the only one confused and left wondering what David was talking about.

Introduction

For many years I have been on a mission to discover the key differences between those people who generate a constant flow of quality sales-leads from their networking activities, and those who get the kind of mediocre results I was getting when I first started business networking. As it turns out I was not alone in being disappointed with the small amount of business generated from networking despite all the time and money invested. Whilst some people seem to do exceptionally well, others seem to put in lots of effort without any great success to speak of. What was I doing wrong? Why was it not happening for me?

My Networking Journey

Even before I had 'officially' started my business full-time I had joined BNI, an international network of business networking breakfasts founded by Dr Ivan Misner. I soaked up as much information as I could and read most of the excellent books written by him. I gave it time but, for some reason, it was just not working for me. I could see how the BNI system worked and that it was clearly working for other members. It was not as if I did not get any business at all. It was just nothing like the level I had imagined or needed. I drifted away from BNI and tried other networking groups with similarly poor results.

Five years later I rejoined my local BNI and this time my membership was much more fruitful. I even won a new client as a result of doing my one-minute presentation when attending as a visitor. There were some small and very important differences in my approach this time around thanks to the insights gained from my research. I went on to also help a number of people in the breakfast group to make big improvements to the sales-leads they generated from their networking. There was no difference in the networking organisation. My approach, however, was different in a number of small but significant ways.

One of the things that first attracted me to study Neuro Linguistic Programming (NLP) was the notion that people who get exceptional results do not necessarily do things dramatically different from the norm. The promise is that if you spend time finding and applying the few key differences to what you are doing in a specific area, then you will start to get similar results. This is referred to as NLP Modelling and I decided to use it to find out how to generate more sales-leads from networking.

Over a number of years I have researched what the successful networkers were doing differently to me. In many cases it was more about the way I thought about networking and Thomas Power, founder and chairman of Ecademy, was a big influence. Once I started to get results for myself and articulate the differences, I began to help others get results too, until I could pinpoint the exact process and a method of facilitating people through that process.

NLP Modelling is simple to describe but not so easy to do in practice. The snag is that people who are excellent at something will rarely have the insight to know what those differences are. They will *think* they know but if you observe them then there will be things they do that they are not even aware of. The other issue is that there is not always one key difference. Some people may be displaying one difference and getting good results. Others may be totally different. This was the case with my research where I discovered several big differences and three small but critical differences. Many people that I have helped get great results were already doing the big differences. Some were even doing one or two of the small differences. It is when all three of the small differences are working well together that magic starts to happen!

The Big Differences That Make All The Difference

Before looking at the critical small differences I think it will be useful just to outline some of the big differences.

PROSPECTING RATHER THAN CONNECTING

Some people go to networking meetings in full sales mode. They broadcast their sales messages, work the room and collect as many business cards as they can. Their approach to following-up on a networking meeting is effectively a cold call. They have met the person and perhaps asked a few 'qualifying' questions but have not taken the time to connect with the person.

I am sure this approach can produce results if done in sufficient numbers but I would have thought it would be more effective to just make a cold call rather than bother with networking.

Networking is about more than just meeting people. It is about connecting with people and developing a spark of a relationship that can grow over time.

FOLLOWING-UP WITH CONNECTIONS

I meet so many people and I do not have the time to follow-up with everyone. By following-up I mean contacting them afterwards and meeting up to get to know each other better. I am sure if a sales-lead had been identified then most would get back in touch and take things further. There will be many people you will meet that do not have an immediate requirement or might never be a suitable customer. Some of these people will still be worth meeting up with.

Once you get to know each other more you could potentially help each other to generate more sales-leads. In networking parlance this type of meeting is referred to as a one-on-one. It is when you start to get to know each other better and is often where the real sales opportunities can arise. Sometimes the sales-lead can come from the other person but more often than not it is with their contacts.

Many people these days are using social media tools like Facebook; Linkedin; Ecademy; and increasingly Twitter to make new connections. I receive requests every day from people wanting to connect with me online. I used to accept their request and never hear from them again. These days I send a message back saying that I would be happy to connect online once we have connected offline. Maybe we will speak via Skype or telephone rather than meeting face-to-face. Some people I meet up with after an initial telephone conversation. The real power of online business networking is when it joins up with the offline world. The online world allows one to keep in touch with so many more people than ever before.

If you network extensively then you will need to be selective about whom you meet up with. I tend to go with my gut instinct. If I see there is some connection and we seem to be enjoying each other's company then I will suggest we meet for coffee. I will also suggest meeting if I think I can connect them with anyone in my network. I would want to get to know them a little better before making the connection just to make sure that both parties would benefit from the introduction.

The same is true with online connection requests. How we connect may vary. What happens once the connection is made is still the same. A decision needs to be made whether or not to follow-up and some of the people that could help you generate the best sales-leads may never become a customer. When you have the three small differences in place then any random meeting could prove fruitful.

NURTURING RELATIONSHIPS

If you want to create a roaring fire the first stage is to light a match. It's what you do with the flame from the match that determines the size and shape of the fire. The way that many network is the equivalent of lighting one match at a time hoping to keep warm from the flame. Nurturing activity is the equivalent of building the fire. It takes time and effort. You will soon learn what type of connection is best to nurture for your needs. I find that if there is good 'chemistry' between us in some shape or form then there is an inherent willingness to help each other. That is why I go for chemistry over logic every time. Some of my best sales-leads can be traced back from chance encounters with people with whom I would once have not bothered to spend time.

Sometimes people start networking and get lucky very quickly. They make a chance connection very soon after starting to network which leads to a big success. For others it takes time. It really depends on what types of sales-leads you are trying to generate. If you are seeking to get a personal introduction to the CEO of a FTSE 100 company then it may take more than meeting someone briefly at a breakfast meeting.

When people make recommendations and referrals to their clients and closest contacts they are effectively putting their reputation on the line. If you mess up with their clients then it could impact upon their personal livelihood. If someone well connected likes you, however, and likes what you do, then they will often advocate you to others and they will help you win business.

Most of my best advocates have not been clients. They are people I have spent time helping in whatever way I can. Often it has been helping them clarify their sales messages or think through a difficult issue. I never expect anything in return from a specific person but I know that if I help enough people then many of them will help me in return in whatever way they can. You will have areas of expertise that you can use to help others, even if it is just the ability to listen without judgment.

I know that many find the unpredictability of this type of networking difficult to handle. It is a leap of faith. I have never met anyone who, when all the other factors are in place, has been disappointed with the results. I see cold calling as very unpredictable. When you phone a number you have no idea whether they will be available, let alone willing, to take your call. Cold Calling becomes more predictable over time with sufficient activity calling on a big enough database. Networking too can become more predictable over time and with sufficient activity. It's the nurturing activity that gets overlooked in the endless search for new connections.

You do not have to give away lots of free things in order to nurture a relationship. Acting as a sounding board or sharing your expertise and know-how when required is often enough. I also find that relationships that start with an introduction from one of my advocates always require a lot less nurturing than those I have started from scratch. Getting your advocates to introduce you to people they know, like, and trust is a good way to rapidly build a quality network from a lead generation perspective.

RANDOM CONNECTIONS

When I talk to others about networking meetings they say things like "Oh that's just full of small businesses, I am looking to do business with large corporates". They are, of course, correct. Most people are running small businesses, but many have large corporate clients that most of us would love to have on our client list. I have met many people through networking meetings who actually work for large corporates but are planning to set up their own business or are running a business in their spare time. These are the exception to the rule and you would never know unless you took the time to get to know them.

I have learnt that taking an open and random approach to networking can reveal some amazing serendipities. I can remember one time trying to find a senior contact in Barclays Bank. I met up with someone running a small business and it turned out that his wife was an ideal connection and he kindly facilitated the introduction. It is only when we put agenda to one side and seek to understand the other person better that such fortuitous happenings occur. If you network with well connected people it is more likely to happen but you never know who someone else is connected with until you take time to get to know them.

EXPECTATIONS

Some people have unrealistic expectations of results from networking. They think that if they say hello, exchange some small talk and thrust a business card in the other person's hand then the people they meet will not only remember them but be happy to immediately start referring business. This is possible but not probable. By the end of the book you are more likely to generate interest from chance encounters, although the best results will come from people with whom we have developed some kind of relationship.

I meet plenty of people who want to have introductions to some of my clients who are proving hard to reach. They expect this to happen without providing a compelling business reason as to why my contact would want to have a conversation with them. As we will see later in the book, there are lots of ways to help facilitate the introduction. There are also many other ways our network can help us to generate quality sales-leads than by just providing referrals. Those same strategies can help you too and we will explore them in chapter eight.

The Small Differences That Make Even More Difference

The big differences above are all major areas to get right to make our networking more productive and there are plenty of excellent books around that help us understand what is required. The following are the few small but vital areas that seem to make a very big difference. These are the ones that made the biggest difference to me personally and the areas I focus on when helping people quickly turnaround their networking fortunes. They can even work without resolving the big differences although all of these areas seem to have an exponential impact.

HOW YOU ARTICULATE WHAT YOU DO

Being able to succinctly describe your target audience, your area of specialisation, and what you can do for your target audience makes a significant difference in generating sales-leads from networking. It seems rather obvious but the root issue of most people who come to me for help is that they have very muddled or confusing business propositions. As a result they struggle to communicate it succinctly in a way others can both understand

and remember. Often the individual thinks they understand their own business and think they are communicating it effectively but what really matters is whether people you speak to "get it".

The way we introduce ourselves is very important and I refer to this later as your networking introduction. What is more important is what lies behind your networking introduction. The introduction is like the tip of the iceberg. What you see above the waterline might look significant but in reality it is dwarfed by what lies beneath the surface.

To get that networking introduction right you need to work on your proposition. By the time you get to the end of chapter six you will have worked through your proposition and you will be able to communicate it in fifteen words or less. The preceding chapters will provide insights and exercises. In chapter six I provide you with a simple template in which to create your proposition statement. My advice is to resist using the template before doing the exercises in the preceding chapters. Doing otherwise will be like trying to drink a cup of coffee by lifting a cup to your lips which has not yet been filled!

TRADING STORIES

I have never met a good sales person who does not use storytelling in some way or another in their sales approach. I have observed many successful networkers using stories in their one-minute introductions to great effect. Including storytelling into your networking approach can make a massive difference in the amount of sales-leads you generate. My work with Espen Holm has enabled me to create a format of storytelling that is particularly effective at generating sales-leads and I will be teaching you this approach in chapter seven. The great thing is that you do not need to be good at telling stories for the approach to work. It is as easy as telling someone what you did at the weekend. In chapter seven you will learn how to construct your own story in a way that amplifies your proposition statement and sticks in the memory of people you talk to.

It is not just about the stories you tell. It is also about taking an interest in the stories of people you network with. You should seek to swap stories with people you meet. As you will learn in chapter two, stories are the oil that make relationships work. Trading stories with people you meet helps to build trust and a bond. As a result people in your network will want to share your stories with people they know. Just showing an interest in other people's stories will significantly accelerate the relationship.

LEVERAGING YOUR EXISTING NETWORK

The third small difference that makes a big difference is how you utilise your existing network. The good news is that for most people their existing network is probably bigger and better than they think. Even if you were to only know one person you have a place to start! In addition to getting to know more people you can get that one person to help you. Have you ever done the exercise of taking one pence and keep on doubling it? It takes a while but at some point the numbers start to get very large. One becomes two. Two becomes four. Four becomes eight and so on. In chapter eight we look at how to leverage your network to generate sales-leads in addition to looking to meet potential clients directly. In Chapter ten we look at how to expand your network in a very time-effective manner.

Making The Most Of Your Sales-Leads

When you start generating lots more sales-leads I want to ensure you maximise your chances of turning them into profitable sales. Chapter nine focuses on recognising when someone expresses an interest and covers a simple sales process. This is for the benefit of readers who are not sales professionals. If you do sell for a living you might want to just read it to check you have a suitable process in place. When I help sales people to close more sales it is often a matter of recognising that a minor but important aspect of the basics is not being done.

Effective Networking

The main thrust of this book is to show you how to generate more sales-leads from networking. The quantity of sales-leads you require will be greatly reduced by the sales process detailed in chapter nine. There are many other things that we can do to minimise the amount of time we need to devote to generating sales-leads and fitting networking into our busy work lives. In the final chapter we will look at ways of being more effective with your time and how to take your networking forward.

Summary

There are many reasons why networking fails to produce results in terms of sales-leads. There are a few key differences that can dramatically improve the productivity of your networking. These are:

- Improving the way in which you articulate what you do;
- the use of storytelling when networking;
- and leveraging the relationships within your existing network.

two

GENERATING SALES-LEADS WHILST YOU SLEEP

When I sat down with David to get to know him better we discussed his business and who would make an ideal client for him. He looked into his coffee cup and stirred it for a while whilst thinking. He then looked up at me and said that his target audience was small and medium sized enterprises. With a little questioning I was able to clarify that it was more the medium sized companies. I could almost hear the penny drop as he realised that the people he most wanted to meet would probably not be attending the networking meetings he attended. Yet many of the people at those meeting could already be doing business with his ideal clients or know someone who is.

David had been busy trying to find a way to make more money from these smaller businesses rather than seeing how he could get introductions to his ideal client.

"I seem to be missing a trick here" he said, excitedly.

Introduction

Wouldn't it be great to have a small army of people generating sales-leads for you without having to pay them a penny? It's not as ridiculous as it sounds. In this chapter I will show you how to do this by tapping into the power of personal recommendation. You will be able to begin duplicating your efforts and make networking much more productive and enjoyable.

People Talk

Did you ever go and see a great film that really moved you? How many people did you tell about it?

Did you ever buy a new product and were so impressed by it that you could not help raving about it to others?

Have you ever heard someone you respect talk enthusiastically about an experience and it has caused you to go and try it?

These are all examples of personal recommendation. It seems it is human nature to want to share good experiences. People around the world are doing it all day, every day. With online social media tools people are not just doing it on a one-on-one basis but in mass volumes.

My wife does not like selling. She does, however, influence a lot of people's buying without realising it or causing it to happen. She just likes helping her friends and work colleagues. When she sees something she likes she talks to other people about it. One of her friends is a talented curtain maker who gets a steady stream of work from people who have been convinced to give her a try after hearing about it from my wife. If my wife was offered money to talk highly about her friend then she would probably not be interested. It's the fact that she is speaking from her heart that makes what she is recommending so powerful. People trust her recommendations because they know, like and trust her.

This behaviour is not exclusive to my wife. It happens everywhere. Wherever people meet they talk and exchange experiences. It happens at the school gates, at the water cooler at work and now on social networking sites like Ecademy, Linkedin, Facebook and Twitter. People trade stories of good experiences, bad experiences, how a product made a difference and so on. And people that listen to these stories are affected by them. These conversations are what really create reputations. It does not matter what your website says, it's what people say behind your back that really counts.

What are you doing to get people talking about you and your products when you are not there? If the answer is 'nothing' then you are missing out on a vital lead generation channel. We need to be tapping into the natural '"word of mouth", the conversations that people you already know are having with their contacts. Doing so can help support your sales efforts, build your credibility, and reduce your competition. Who would you rather spend your money with to clean your house? Someone whose name you got out of the Yellow Pages or someone who came highly recommended by the people you know, like, and trust?

It seems the more risk that is involved in a purchasing decision, the more we turn to our network for recommendations. We will be looking at how to work with human nature and the power of "word of mouth" stories to help us generate leads from networking. The great thing is that as a result of the work we will be doing, you can get better results from all your marketing channels.

People Tell Stories

People love stories. It is part of our human psyche and tradition. Long before writing was invented, stories were the way in which learning was passed on. Before the days of book publication, mass media and the movies, there was a very strong culture of storytelling in many countries, and it is especially prevalent in the histories of Ireland, Denmark and Norway. One thing I discovered some years ago is that storytelling is one thing that top sales people seem to have in common. For many it is so natural to them that they do not even realise they do it. It's just part of their make-up.

There is a type of story that most of us tell when we meet friends and family. We probably have never considered it to be a story because it does not begin with "once upon a time...". We share them with one another almost daily at work, at home, at the school gates. Whenever we get asked questions like "What did you do at the weekend?' or "How was your holiday?' or even "How's it going?" We often respond with anecdotes, which are, of course, a type of story in themselves. At dinner parties people will share anecdotes and often one anecdote will spark another. One person will talk about a funny incident during their trek in Peru and another person might recount a funny incident that occurred on a holiday in another country.

Some people are really masterful at telling elaborate stories, and are known as "raconteurs". The anecdotes that most of us share in our day-today conversations, however, tend to be natural and understated, and it is this type of story that you will be using when talking about your products and services, and when sharing your customer success stories.

Swapping Stories

When doing my workshops I normally start off just by asking people to get together in small groups and share with each other how they came to be working at their company or how they came to start their business. Everyone is relaxed and enjoys the process. I point this out to the room and that they should be telling their success stories in exactly the same way; Natural and understated. The act of telling your networking stories should be no different to recounting to a friend what you got up to at the weekend.

Trading stories with people you meet is not just about you delivering your sales messages through stories. One of the easiest ways I have found of developing rapport with someone is to ask them their story. If you ever get faced with a frosty prospect and you want to break the ice simply ask them their story. Ask them how they came to start their business or how they came to be in their current job. They will enjoy the process and provided you are interested then any tension will begin to melt away rapidly. If all you get from this book is to tell your success stories and ask people you meet about their success stories, you will make a massive step forward in developing networking relationships.

It's Not Who You Know

When you meet people for the first time, do you see them in terms of whether they would make a good customer or not? That is a very limited view of networking in my opinion. I see people at network meetings all the time 'working the room'. You speak to them and whilst they are talking to you they are busy looking over your shoulder deciding on their next victim. Working the room is a valid approach if you are just looking for potential clients from people in the room. The problem is that when I ask such people who their ideal clients are, they are not in the room. They want bread but they settle for crumbs.

I am always amazed at the connections people have. Until you get to know them you might never find out that they are married to a potential client or play golf with someone you have been trying to reach by more conventional methods. People in business normally have between 200 and 400 contacts and some considerably more. If you go into a room of 100 business people – even if they are just the owners of small businesses – then there are between 20,000 and 40,000 connections in that room alone.

If you had access to that many contacts do you think at least some of them could want your products and services? If we want access to all those connections we will need to change our approach to networking from just working the room. In addition to looking for clients we also need to be on the lookout for introducers. Every client could become an introducer but some of your best potential introducers may never become clients.

Networking Meetings Are A Good Place To Start

I meet so many people that say things like "I do not go to those networking meetings because they are full of small businesses". It is ironic when people from small businesses say this! What they are really saying is that they want to network in places where people like them do not go! If you feel that way then I understand exactly how you feel. I felt the same way until I learnt that plenty of people I was meeting at the small business networks were doing business with my ideal clients. What is more, I discovered that many of them first started working with their sizeable clients through a recommendation from someone they had met at a networking meeting. I began to realise that if I could get people I know to introduce me to people they know then I could massively replicate my lead generation efforts.

Just imagine that you had a small army of people looking out for sales opportunities for you. Especially people already working with your ideal clients in some capacity. For example, they provide them with things like printing, training, consultancy, IT services, web design. They spot an opportunity that could be ideal for you and start talking to their client about you and how you could help them achieve what they want. As a result their client's PA calls you to make an appointment to meet with you. The meeting goes well and what is more you find that there is no competition. Wouldn't that be great?

Pigeons In The Park

When I was learning to network I was taught to do so as if I were feeding pigeons in the park. It is an analogy that I have followed with great success and now teach to others who want help to generate more sales-leads from networking. I have turned it into a little story to help make the point.

It was Peter's sixth birthday and as a special treat his father had taken him to the local park to feed the pigeons. Peter had heard from his school friends that it was possible to have pigeons eat from your hand and that is what Peter intended to do today. His father handed him a few slices of bread and clutching tightly he began to run towards a group of hungry looking pigeons shouting:

"Dinner time! Dinner time! Come and get some lovely bread!" As Peter approached, all the pigeons flew away. The more he tried the more pigeons left the park. Peter finally bowed his head, bit his lip and began to sob. His father came over and put his arm around the little boy and said:

"Here Peter, let me show you how it's done."

His father broke off a few pieces of bread and slowly began sprinkling them on the floor and just ignored the pigeons. After a little while a couple of curious pigeons came forward and began to peck cautiously at the bread, all the time checking to make sure it was safe. Gradually the pigeons could sense it was safe and came a little closer eating the crumbs as they went, all the time checking for danger, poised to fly at any moment. The father gently lowered his hand very carefully and opened his palm to display the crumbs. Before long one pigeon eased forward and began to peck at the crumbs in his hand. Then another pigeon came forward followed by another and another. Soon the whole area around the father and son was covered in pigeons all flying in from the local neighbourhood.

If you want to develop great business referrals and business prospects then you need to make sure you do not scare people away by coming across as a pushy sales person. Be natural and others will feel comfortable talking to you. These are the very people that could connect you to your biggest ever piece of business. This may not be easy to tell when you first meet them. You need to treat everyone you meet with the same respect you would if they were providing you with a regular stream of sales-leads. You never know who will become your biggest and most important advocate.

Working The Room, With A Difference

When I first came across the notion of "working the room" I have to say I was not impressed. I value my integrity and I found the prospect of meeting people and pretending to like them so that they would introduce me to their clients a little distasteful. I also did not like when I was on the receiving end of being "worked". Typically this involved someone talking at me whilst looking over my shoulder for someone better to talk to. They would then proceed to thrust their business card into my hand before moving on to their next victim!

When I now meet people at a networking meeting I am not thinking about what I can sell them. I am not even trying to find out who they know. The only thing that matters is whether there is some mutual connection and I would like to invest time and energy in getting to know them better. I spend most of our conversation talking about them and seeing if there is any potential to put them in touch with people I know. I generally like to get to know people well before making introductions to clients but matchmaking them with people in my network can potentially help them and my other contacts.

For example, I have someone I know who specialises in environmentally friendly printing and he works with many environmental charities. I met someone at a meeting who specialised in providing consulting services to charities. I judged they would get on well together and offered to make the introduction knowing that they would be pleased and that it could help both to generate sales-leads for each other.

A different way of working the room is to look for people you have some kind of chemistry with and with whom you would be happy to meet again for coffee, a drink, or even dinner. The strange thing is that by using the strategies in this book and not seeking to generate leads I end up generating interest when I happen to meet someone who would be an ideal client.

Getting Recommended

Imagine you have a client with whom you have a brilliant trusted relationship and who values your opinion. They are very important in terms of your personal income. They ask you to recommend someone to help them in a particular area because your previous recommendations have been first class. What would it take for you to be prepared to recommend someone else to this person?

The dilemma is that you want to please your client and each good recommendation increases the chance of them coming back to you when they have a problem – the holy grail of any would be "trusted advisor". A bad recommendation, however, could undo all the good work you have done and potentially put a strain on the relationship. Anybody recommending you could well be going through the same dilemma. They could have lots to gain by recommending you but perhaps even more to lose. It is no wonder it takes a little work to get the relationship into a place where they feel comfortable recommending you.

In my experience, it takes three elements for people to feel comfortable advocating you to their best contacts. They need to know you, like you, and trust you. You may have heard this before so I will go through each to ensure you fully understand what each involves.

Know You

When you meet someone at a networking meeting, or you exchange a friend request online, it is generally done at a very superficial level. Effective networkers will seize the initiative to take that initial introduction to the next level by inviting the other person to meet up and get to know each other better. In networking circles such a meeting is commonly referred to as a "one-to-one" or one-on-one meeting. Ideally this should be in person but if I have met someone already then the telephone works well for me. Some people will recommend you without ever getting to know you better but you often find it's because someone they know has recommended you.

If I meet someone at a meeting where I think there could be some mutual interest I will ask for their card and suggest we meet for coffee so that I can better understand what they do. It should be a two way exchange. If you take an interest in what they do then they will almost always reciprocate. Expect a one-to-one meeting to last about one hour. That should leave about thirty minutes for each person. To get the most from these meetings you will need to be able to clearly articulate what you do and back it up with some pertinent example stories. I will be helping you to craft these in later chapters. I always take responsibility to better understand the other person's business if it is not clear. I will ask them for examples of an ideal client and what they did for them.

As well as knowing you personally they also need to know what you do well enough to be able to look out for opportunities and explain it to others in simple terms. It is safe to assume that if you cannot clearly articulate what you do to others then potential introducers will struggle to pass on that information to people they know. They may also be justified in assuming that you will struggle to communicate effectively when sitting in front of their client.

Like You

Whilst it is possible that someone who does not like you will recommend you based on your skills or product it's highly unlikely. Most products and services have plenty of alternatives. I can remember meeting someone who had a great telecoms product but I found him incredibly difficult to get on with. I normally get on with most people but found him a little strange. He got very upset that I ended up recommending someone else who sold the same product. It was because this new person took the time to get to know me and establish a relationship with me.

Your potential introducers will assume that if they do not like you then their contacts will not like you either. During your initial meeting and subsequent one-to-one meeting you will need to make yourself more likeable. This is best done by taking a sincere interest in the other person and getting them talking about themselves and sharing their stories. Looking for chemistry is effectively checking to see whether you seem to get on together. If there is no chemistry then it is probably going to be a waste of time meeting up.

Trust You

Knowing and liking is important but trust is critical. Unless they trust you with their clients and contacts then you will not get any quality introductions. One level of trust is whether they believe what you say. There seems to be a general perception that pushy sales people cannot be trusted, so if you behave like one then you run the risk of not being trusted and of the other person discounting everything you say. Just be natural and authentic and most people will trust you. Expect some people you meet to be watching to see how consistent you are. I remember one person I know changing their business model four times in a year. He would make a lot of noise each time and by the fourth time he had lost any credibility he had with people in his network. Could you imagine recommending someone who you cannot rely on to be doing the same thing a week later?

The word "credibility" relates directly to believability. The more consistent we are in our sales messages and the way we behave and interact, the more believable we become. We also need to be consistent in what we think, what we say, and what we do. People will definitely be checking whether you do what you say. This is why it is so important, if you are likely to be late for a meeting, to call and let them know.

I once recommended someone to a client for a specific need. I knew him, liked him, and thought I could trust him. Whilst he was honest and good at what he did, he proceeded to start trying to sell things into my client that I provide. He had not banked on the strength of the relationships I build up. The client told me straight away. My client was not impressed. I was not impressed and he never got another referral from me again. He had demonstrated that he could not be trusted.

The Emotional Bank Account

In his excellent book *The 7 Habits of Highly Effective People*, Stephen R Covey uses a metaphor of an emotional bank account. The more we deposit into the account with people the more we can potentially withdraw. If you want something when networking and you have only just met the person you are like someone with no credit history going to the bank manager asking for an overdraft. The easiest way to build up a balance on your account with that person is to help them out in some way. One way to do this is what I call "matchmaking". This is where I introduce someone I have just met to a contact within my existing network. I do this when I feel both parties could potentially be of benefit to each other. The great thing is that if the match goes well then not only do they each benefit but it also builds my emotional bank account with both people. I would not introduce them to a client at this stage but someone who I know will get on with them and could help them in some way.

Giving quality referrals will probably add more to an emotional bank account than anything else. If you can help your contacts win some business then, in my experience, they will bend over backwards to reciprocate.

Networking Heaven, Networking Hell

There is a nice description I read once of Heaven and Hell. It describes Hell as a place where people are seated around a dining table, starving, and yet on the table before them is an array of sumptuous food. The people at the table can smell the beautiful aromas and yet no one is able to eat. They are all starving despite being in the midst of so much food. On closer inspection each person has a long ladle strapped to each arm. They are unable to bend their arms and the ladle is too long to reach their mouth. There is much wailing and gnashing of teeth!

The definition of Heaven is actually identical to Hell in every respect. The same dining table and the same food. The same ladles strapped to each person's arms. The difference is that people around the table are feeding each other rather than just trying to feed themselves.

I love this as an analogy and it is especially appropriate for networking. It sums up how we can generate all the sales-leads we need by helping other people generate sales-leads. Help is not always direct introductions to clients but indirect introductions to people we know who later go on to make introductions to potential clients. The more you help others the more they tend to help you back. Not everyone does but when you use chemistry as a qualifier for making new contacts then the chances are they will be suitably like-minded.

Keeping to the analogy, it is easy to sit there and think:

"If someone feeds me then I will feed them back."

Perhaps that is what causes the Hell in the first place. Everyone sitting there waiting for someone else to make the first move. I have learnt that if you want something to happen then it pays to be the one to seize the initiative and make the first move. I find that people like to meet up for coffee but they don't always think of asking.

Summary

When you build up a network you create the potential for word of mouth referrals. This is more likely to happen when people know you, like you, and trust you. Take the initiative to meet people for one-on-one meetings if you find you have something in common. Use these meetings to trade stories and build your emotional bank account with the other person. Do this by seeking to understand them and how you can potentially help them such as matchmaking them with someone who will also be able to help them.

three

DEVELOPING YOUR APPEAL

I could see the excitement in David's eyes now as he contemplated the possibilities. Everyone he had already met and everyone he would meet in the future could not only become a potential client but also an introducer for him. This would make it much easier to generate the kind of sales-leads he really needed to build a successful business. By working with them he would replicate his sales efforts many times over and he would have many people looking and listening out for opportunities for him, even when he was busy working with his clients.

"So Richard," David said to me thinking aloud "I guess if I expect these people to be out looking for opportunities for me then I need to let them know what, specifically, to look out for."

Introduction

I meet so many people who have amazing products and services that can be of massive benefit to their ideal clients. Yet they seem unable to articulate to those who would make ideal clients, just how their existing clients benefit from working with them, and why those potential clients should want to work with them rather than their competitors. In this chapter I will take you through the **APPEAL** framework which is designed to help you craft compelling sales messages to use whilst networking.

What Are You Selling?

When I was at Cranfield School of Management many years ago we were taught a saying that I expect anyone who has ever studied marketing will have heard a version of:

People do not buy a drill, they buy a hole.

At the time I thought these were just clever words. It took me a long time to realise the profoundness of the statement, which alludes to the very thing that, in my experience, holds the key to any sale: buying motivation. Selling becomes so much easier when you know what is driving their buying behaviour or what would motivate them to start thinking about buying.

To understand the buying motivation of someone buying a drill, therefore, we need to take it one stage further. We need to discover *why* those people want to buy a hole in the first place! It could be for a number of reasons, such as:

- To hang a family portrait on the wall
- To put up a shelf to show off their child's sporting trophies
- To make a trellis for their beautiful garden
- To batten down the windows to protect their house from a tornado

The important thing to realise is that these people buying a drill did not buy one just for the sake of it. They bought it for a specific reason. There are often alternative options to any buying decision. Let's take the example of a mother wanting a shelf to show off her child's sporting trophies. Here are some alternative options to buying a drill:

- Use a special glue
- Pay someone to put up the shelf
- Borrow a drill from a neighbour
- Buy a shelving unit
- Buy a glass display cabinet

Of course we know that there are enough people around needing a hole, for whatever reason, to sustain a market for hole making devices. If we focus too much on the drill we risk losing sight of its potential to add value to those who buy one. In the same way, it is a common sales mistake to focus too much on what we are selling rather than on how potential clients will benefit.

It is very useful, therefore, for us to take time to understand the buying motivation for our target audience. If you were a craftsman making carved wooden display cabinets then it is worth looking at the reasons behind your customers' decisions to buy and using that information to shape your marketing focus and sales messages. In networking conversations people seem to be more interested in hearing about why your customers bought your cabinet and how they felt about it when it was in their home, rather than hearing about the craftsmanship and the quality of the wood.

Sell What People Are Buying

Do you know what your ideal prospects are looking for? Are they looking for a solution? Are you trying to sell something that solves a problem your target audience does not realise they have? This whole area around who the target audience is and what they are looking for is normally at the root of problems generating sales-leads, especially from networking.

Does someone who is struggling to get things done because they are too busy actually know they need a Virtual Assistant? Or are they just wishing for a bit more time to get things done? It is hard to say and the only way to find out is to get to know your target audience better and understand what they are actually buying. Once we gain those insights then it becomes easier to formulate and articulate our sales messages in a way that can be understood by prospects and potential introducers.

It is an important mental shift to go from thinking "How do I sell more of my products and services" to "Who would want to buy my products and services and why?" Discovering this information is what makes crafting sales messages so much easier. If people are looking for something specific and you indicate that you may be able to help them, then why would they not be open to having a brief conversation? A sales-lead is really only an expression of interest. Your job is to get the right people to express an interest in your products and services and that is more likely to happen if you know what your target audience are really looking for.

Market research is an important part of business planning. It is an area often overlooked when small businesses set up. They are too focused on their products and services rather than discovering their target audience and the motivation to buy. Your existing or past clients can provide valuable market research. They have spent money with you and that counts for a lot.

Doing The Groundwork

The **APPEAL** framework will help you better understand what your prospects are buying and why. It will also provide the raw materials from which you can craft your sales messages and stories. Think of it as the foundations for your sales messages. When building a house the foundations seem to take forever. Once the foundations are in place then the process of building a house is very simple. The same is true for creating sales messages. There are six key areas that provide the foundations of your networking sales messages. I am using the mnemonic **APPEAL** which stands for:

A – Audience

P – Pain

P – Proposition

E – Example

A – Advantage

L – Links

AUDIENCE

Your target audience is the most important part of the groundwork as all things flow from the target audience. We will be getting to know them in much more detail. If you consider your target audience as small and medium sized companies, or businesses in the motor trade then that is too generalised. What we want is to start to build up a picture of the specific person you want to be connected to. We will look at splitting out your target audience into groups based on their primary buying motivation and seeking to understand more about them as people. Your target audience represents your ideal clients.

For example, the target audience for this book I think of as the 'frustrated networker'. It is someone who is sold on the idea of networking for the purposes of finding clients and has invested a lot of time and money into networking but is failing to get the quality sales-leads they seek. The person could be self employed, run their own business or be part of a bigger organisation. The important thing is that they feel frustrated with the results they are getting from networking and want to learn how to be more effective.

I am sure this book will possibly **APPEAL** to some people outside my target audience. Your products and services will also have a wider potential audience too. When you focus your sales messages to specific buying motivations of specific target audiences then they become much more compelling. Trying to **APPEAL** to multiple buying motivations causes sales messages to get diluted and as a result they have a reduced impact.

The way in which I help clients gain insights so quickly is by creating these sub-groups and exploring the buying motivation of each. I call them Customer Archetypes; we will work on these in chapter four.

PAIN

Once you know your Customer Archetypes then you can start to get a sense of their relevant problems and the pain those problems are causing them. You should also get insights into what they might already have done about it. Do they have any sense of what a solution might look like? Are they looking for something in particular and cannot find it? Or maybe the cause of pain is a consequence of having unreliable suppliers. We just do not know until we first break down our target audience and explore the pain of each Customer Archetype. When we get to crafting your example stories you will see that pain is what will make your stories so powerful in generating sales-leads.

For example, Janice was getting really fed up. Her seminars were all well attended and everyone left saying they found the content very interesting. Yet she was doing the seminars to generate sales-leads and when she looked at the business she had generated from them she was wondering whether it was all a waste of time. After going through the **APPEAL** sales messaging process and adding stories into her presentation she started generating quality sales-leads every time she ran the seminar.

Previously her seminars were too theoretical. The stories breathed life into the experience for the audience. Now they could relate to the pain being experienced by the people in the stories and their situations. They sit there thinking:

"Wow, that is just like me! And they managed to solve it? ... maybe it's worth speaking to this lady to find out more."

PROPOSITION

The word "proposition" has quite a few meanings, so I would like to begin by defining it in the context of this book as your offering to your target audience. It does not necessarily mean specific products and services. It's about what you are proposing to do for your target audience in exchange for money. It's a very important concept to grasp in sales.

For example:

> *The proposition of this book is: If you buy this book I will show you how to generate more sales-leads from networking.*

The proposition is really about how you are able to take away the pain of your target audience. The primary buying motivation may be different for each Customer Archetype but your proposition is likely to remain constant unless you design a range of products and services specific to one particular Customer Archetype.

When I work with very small businesses I often get them to focus, in the short-term, on one Customer Archetype and they end up developing brand new propositions that offer an exciting range of products and services for that group of people. With services that is easy to do. With products you might add additional services around the products to address the specific pain. The product remains the same. What changes is how it is applied to solve a specific problem.

Your proposition is going to be an important factor in how you describe what you do to others. The aim is to describe specifically what you do for your clients in fifteen words or less, which we will do together in chapter six so that you have a proposition statement that stands out from the crowd and gets remembered.

EXAMPLE

Stories are one of the best kept secrets of top sales people. There are many different story types that have different applications from a sales perspective. I call the story that helps generate sales-leads an *example story* because it provides an example of how an ideal client has benefited from a product or service.

The example stories you create will illuminate your proposition statement and help people you talk to "see what you mean." Once you have a clear idea of your target audience, their pain, and your proposition, you are better able to go through your customer success stories and make them both compelling and memorable. It is not enough for us to be able to tell our stories. We want our potential introducers to be able to repeat them when they meet a potential client.

The example stories are designed to be short enough to use at breakfast meetings where you have a minute to introduce yourself to other people in the room. You will be able to introduce yourself, deliver your proposition statement and your example story; all in less than a minute.

I use example stories all the time when I meet people for a one-to-one meeting. I do not even think about it consciously anymore. It has become part of my unconscious behaviour and the same will happen to you over time once you get into the habit. Many of the top sales people whom I have met were unaware that they used stories as an important aspect of their sales approach. I have even helped some make their example stories even more powerful by adopting the approach in chapter seven.

You may have lots of different example stories for the same proposition. When making a movie there is only one plot. The example story details may change but the plot remains the same. You might even do a different example story for each Customer Archetype so that when you meet someone you just tell them the example story appropriate to their particular archetype. The response you are looking for is: "That is just like me!" or "I know someone just like that!"

ADVANTAGE

There is one question you will definitely need to address when you are selling in general and when speaking to potential introducers in particular. It is the "Why you?" question. There are probably many people who, like you, can potentially solve a client's problems, so you need to identity your point of difference. People will not normally ask you but letting them know can make a big difference to the quantity of sales-leads you generate.

Let's suppose you are a life coach and you are looking for more sales-leads from someone in your network who is in an excellent position to refer business to you. She knows you, likes you, and trusts you. However, she knows, likes, and trusts another twenty life coaches. Why should she recommend you rather than the other twenty people she already knows?

What we are seeking here is what sets you apart from your competitors; your key point of difference. Your product could be identical but you have a specific area of expertise or experience in a particular market. The advantage is really about the edge you have over your competitors with your specific target audience. It is an important insight to gain because it will affect your proposition statement and the example stories you select to tell. That is why we cover it in chapter six and show you why it is better to specialise when networking than to generalise. Rather than looking for a *unique selling point* you will develop your *unique networking proposition*.

An example is a Virtual Assistant with whom I worked who was very much a generalist. She was getting nowhere near the level of business she wanted and was struggling to differentiate herself from other Virtual Assistants. We went through the **APPEAL** process and decided her area of specialisation was helping people who want the benefits of social media but who do not know where to start and do not have the time to find out, let alone set it up and manage it. This was her area of maximum credibility and she had lots of good example stories of taking away her clients pain. By emphasizing her advantage she quickly started to pick up more clients from her network and her business fortunes were transformed as a result. Interestingly, once she had started working with a client she easily managed to successfully cross-sell other less differentiated services to them; the very same services she previously struggled to sell.

LINKS

The big sales-lead generation potential of a business network is not just the people within your network but their links to other people. When you take a random approach to networking then people you meet may not be an ideal client but they may be linked to people who are or, more than likely, who can help you reach them. You will find your networking so much more productive in terms of sales-lead generation when you seek to leverage the links of people within your network rather than just seeing everyone as a potential client. Top sales people know that it takes a lot less effort to close a sale from a warm introduction than from a cold call.

A good example of someone effectively using links is an IT consultant I worked with. His target audience was IT Directors of large organisations. His proposition statement at the time was helping large organisations reduce IT costs without reducing service levels. We identified that his target audience was newly appointed IT Directors who want to make their mark. They tended to be less defensive and looking for new ideas to make a big impact. Together we went through his links and he identified that interim IT Directors would be a good contact, especially if they are between assignments. He focused his short-term networking on getting connections to good Interim IT Directors. He was amazed at how many connections he actually got. They were all happy to meet him as he was able to provide them with fresh ideas and potentially help them find their next assignment.

He quickly managed to schedule around thirty meetings with interim IT Directors, some of whom were newly in position. The sales-leads started to come in before he managed to see everyone on his list.

In chapter eight, I will show you several different ways in which you can approach your existing network to use their links to help you immediately start generating more sales-leads

Summary

The **APPEAL** framework helps us to clarify the foundations of our business. By working through each of the six areas (Audience, Pain, Proposition, Example, Advantage and Links) we can more easily craft compelling sales messages and reach out to our target audience.

four

CLIENTS FROM HEAVEN

Most of the clients that David was working with were not right for him. He resented the fact that they kept on changing their mind on projects and he was hardly making any money from them. He felt like he was being taken for a ride. At the same time he felt grateful that he was at least getting some income, even if it was nowhere near enough to survive on.

David had worked with a couple of clients whom he really enjoyed working with. He wanted to find more of them and be able to turn away the type of people that always seemed to cause him headaches and sleepless nights. His ideal clients always had interesting projects and they valued his expertise. They also were happy to pay higher rates and they did not require major effort on his part to pay their bill.

David knew the type of clients he liked to work with when he met them but had no idea how to put that into words.

Introduction

In understanding how to generate more sales-leads from networking, the target audience is normally the best place to start. When asking people about their target audience , the reply is all too often something vague like: "SMEs" (small and medium sized enterprises) or "Anyone who can afford my services!" Even when it is something more specific like: "Finance Directors of Software companies" there is still massive room for improvement.

In this chapter we will look at the first stage of the **APPEAL** framework which is *Audience*. We will be getting a better understanding of your ideal clients by defining your Customer Archetypes.

Introducing Customer Archetypes

I first coined the term Customer Archetype to help a specific client distinguish between customers he wanted to attract and those he should avoid. I know it sounds a little unusual but my client, the owner of a web design agency, confessed to me:

"I hate my clients! They want a website for next to nothing, are never satisfied and what's more they upset all my staff."

His lead generation efforts were attracting what I call his "Clients from Hell". When we do business with the wrong clients, especially when it comes to services, it all so often ends in tears. What this client desperately wanted was to identify and start to find his "Clients from Heaven".

We started to look at his current and former clients and group them based on their buying motivation. For completeness we also added in regular prospects who made enquiries but from whom he had not won the business. My client began to realise that he already had some clients from Heaven. They were a really good fit to his business, a joy to work with, appreciated the value they were getting and were happy to pay for the service. Unfortunately they were in the minority. We gave each different group a name and worked out how to attract more of the good ones and qualify-out the undesirable ones. That is the purpose of discovering your Customer Archetypes. It is an incredibly quick and effective way to gain clarity. Working with the results of that exercise led my client to quickly start winning more of his ideal clients and weeding out the undesirable ones.

The Customer Archetypes technique is nothing new. Consumer stereotyping is used widely in mass marketing; "Mondeo Man" and the "YUPPIE" are just two examples. It helps marketers to profile segments of the market that are worth targeting.

Where the Customer Archetypes approach differs is how it focuses on primary buying motivation and begins with your own client base. The insights that you gain from your Customer Archetypes help you to better understand your clients and prospects and what they are looking for. They also provide a rich source of example stories to help shape your sales messages.

Customer Archetypes For New Businesses

But what if you do not have any clients yet? Whilst it does work better with businesses that have some clients, it is possible to create Customer Archetypes based on a particular market before setting-up in business. One client found herself a mentor with experience in the market. I have also worked with a number of people who have purchased a franchise. We were able to get input from their franchisors.

The golden rule for me is that if you cannot come up with any customer example stories then you probably have some work to do to build up your credibility. This is where you can go to your network for help. They are more likely to give you the benefit of the doubt and help you get established. Arrange to meet them for coffee to show them what you are doing and ask for their advice. This should not be a sales pitch. You are asking their advice on how to find your first clients. Perhaps say you are willing to offer a free or greatly reduced service in return for a case study.

When I first started as a Sales Consultant I had a lot of experience but no clients. For six months I tapped into my network to find people to work with who I would not charge but who would provide testimonials and speak to potential clients. They became my first stories. They allowed me to get started and I did not begrudge not being paid as the credibility and referability was worth so much more. I still recall my very first paying client with great fondness!

Naming Your Customer Archetypes

The magic of Customer Archetypes happens once you give them a name. It is not a difficult exercise to identify and name them. There are typically five or six Customer Archetypes. Attendees on my Master-class manage to define theirs in less than ten minutes. The names make it easier to start distinguishing differences between the groups. The groups then provide a simple vehicle for taking a more flexible sales approach both to generating sales-leads and converting them into cash in the bank. We can tailor our sales messages and stories to specific Customer Archetypes. We can also adopt different closure strategies for different Customer Archetypes.

An example: One of my first clients with whom I used the Customer Archetypes approach provides public training courses for budding massage therapists. She was generating lots of sales-leads but was frustrated that despite all her marketing efforts, only around 20% of the enquiries ended up on her courses. The owner of the business was actually closing a much higher proportion but she relied on the office staff to handle enquiries. She wanted a simple way for her office staff to know what to do to close the sale.

We went through the typical type of people making enquiries and came up with...

- The ready-to-gos
- The full-timers
- The part-timers
- The warm and fuzzies
- The dreamers

THE READY-TO-GOS

The primary buying motivation for this group was to gain the skills and get a certificate so that they could start trading as a massage therapist. They probably already had their business cards made up and had found a place to run their massage clinics. They were literally ready-to-go. All they needed was to find a suitable training course and that was why they made the enquiry. These were the people that mostly booked onto their training courses at that time.

THE FULL-TIMERS

The primary buying motivation behind this group is that they were looking for a career change. We could have called them "The career changers" but the client wanted to distinguish the full-timers and part-timers. I imagined someone from this group sitting in an office watching the clock ticking slowly and thinking:

> *"I hate my job! I want to do something else – what could I do? I had a massage once and I would love to be able to do that for a living…"*

So they make the enquiry and ask for more information. Their big worry, however, is whether they will be able to earn enough money to pay their mortgage.

The office staff were trained to find out which Customer Archetype they were speaking to and if it was a full-timer they would inject into the conversation something like:

> *"We speak to a lot of people who are looking for a career change. They are often worrying whether they will earn enough to pay the mortgage. What we suggest is that you start off on a part-time basis and then, when you develop regular clients, you can make the decision whether to give up your job and go full time."*

They would invite them to an open evening where they could meet and talk to clients who had successfully gone through a similar process. They would also "pencil-in" the person onto a course, to be confirmed once they had been to the open evening.

Can you see that talking to the full-timers about the quality of the training will not be as attractive as talking to them about a career in massage therapy and how to make it work?

THE PART-TIMERS

This Customer Archetype had a primary buying motivation of earning extra money. The person probably had a full-time job and was thinking of becoming a massage therapist to earn extra money. This could have been for a variety of reasons such as being able to afford a family holiday, save for a deposit on a house, or maybe simply to make ends meet. The person would probably be a little worried about whether it could work for her.

The office staff member was trained to say something like:

> *"We speak to a lot of people looking to earn extra income in their spare time. They often want to know what is involved in finding clients. We cover this on our courses and what we recommend is that you first come along to our public open-day and meet some people who are successfully running a part-time massage business. You can ask them questions and check it is still something you want to do."*

She would then agree to pencil-in that person for the course, to be confirmed after the open-day. They found that if they pencilled-in people to the training they were more likely to go ahead. Some did cancel but overall bookings were up significantly.

Can you see how attracting this Customer Archetype would require a different approach to the full-timers?

THE WARM AND FUZZIES

This group did not really have a buying motivation. The image and marketing of the business seemed to attract a certain type of person who "liked the vibe" and energy. They came along to the open evenings and actually made the event buzz which helped to encourage the main Customer Archetypes to book. The business owner knew that despite people from this group not buying, they were good ambassadors and recommended their training to people who do buy. They were valuable advocates and needed to be looked after. The approach agreed with the office staff, was to invite them on the open evenings but not to bother trying to book them in unless they specifically asked.

THE DREAMERS

This group also had no buying motivation and were generally seen as "time wasters". Their motivation to make the enquiry was similar to the full-timers but when they were asked what motivated them to make the enquiry, their answer would be incoherent. The instruction to office staff was to be polite and just give dates and prices of the courses. Dreamers rarely ever took things any further.

ARCHETYPE	PRIMARY BUYING MOTIVATION
Ready-to-gos	Skills Training
Full-timers	Career Change
Part-timers	Earn extra money
Warm and fuzzies	None but good advocates
Dreamers	None

Testing Your Customer Archetypes

Once you have chosen your Customer Archetypes the big test is to go through your client list and start putting specific client names against each Customer Archetype. If you do not know your clients well enough to understand what motivated them to originally purchase from you then this could be a good time to find out! I recently worked with a larger sized client and they commissioned me to phone twenty clients and ask them about their original decision to buy and the problems that they were trying to solve. It was something they could have easily done themselves but they were too busy and wanted to get an independent opinion.

When you begin to put names against your Customer Archetypes they start to come alive and become more tangible. You can start putting specific client faces against each Customer Archetype to make them more real. This also makes it much easier to communicate with them. When going through the process of assigning names you could find some that do not fit any of your Customer Archetypes. This could indicate that you may need to go back and refine your Customer Archetypes.

CLIENTS AND CONSUMERS

When defining your Customer Archetypes it is important to distinguish between the customer and the consumer. For example, an executive coach may work with several different types of executive but unless they are paying for their own coaching they are not the customer. The correct person would be the one ultimately paying the bill for the coaching like the HR Director or the CEO.

PRIMARY MOTIVATION

It is possible to create your Customer Archetypes with any form of difference. I have seen some people create their Customer Archetypes from bases such as attitudes, readiness to change, and marital status. As a technique it's great for gaining clarity. In the context of sales-lead generation we want to know those details but the thing that will allow us to gain their attention is their primary buying motivation.

The primary motivator is the thing that is predominantly driving the buying behaviour. The reality is that many will have multiple motivators but the primary one is the *deal breaker*. It is the one foremost in their mind and that varies by person. Sales messages will find fertile ground when addressing the primary motivation. Using multiple motivations in the same message is like watering down an espresso coffee. You can still taste the coffee but it does not have the same impact.

DEFINING YOUR CUSTOMER ARCHETYPES

There are several ways to approach the defining of your Customer Archetypes. One of the simplest ways is to choose a category of something like flowers and start comparing your clients and prospects to them. For example, you might have The Roses, The Sunflowers etc. You then say why a certain client is like a certain flower and from there determine their primary buying motivation.

For example, "John from XYZ Ltd is like a Rose. He is an excellent client although difficult to handle. His primary buying motivation is reliability. You only get one shot with John. Let him down and you are history!"

I can remember vividly a lady on one of my public Master-classes who was really passionate about shoes. Each of her Customer Archetypes was a different type of shoe. For example, one group were called the brogues, another the stilettos and so on.

My preferred approach when working with clients is to choose a name that says something about the buying motivation. Here are the Customer Archetypes we identified for the retail re-sellers of a well known sewing machine company:

ARCHETYPE	PRIMARY BUYING MOTIVATION
Money Savers	Save money by making things
Fashionistas	Make their own stylish clothes
Creatives	Creative outlet
Part-time Entrepreneurs	Earn extra money
Professionals	Earn a living

Case Study

To help you define your Customer Archetypes I am providing you with an ongoing case study that we will follow through each aspect of the **APPEAL** framework stage.

The case study is based on work done with a sound engineer called Gary who provides services and rents audio visual products to event organisers. Gary has worked with sound and audio visual equipment for as long as he can remember and he is passionate about events and putting on a fabulous show that everyone enjoys and raves about. He knows how the small details can make or break a show and is meticulous in his attention to detail.

Gary has a regular and profitable clientele who love working with him and his small team. The profit from his business is only sufficient to allow himself a small salary. He is fed up with struggling to make ends meet after so many years in business and has decided to go for it, embrace sales, and start generating significantly more regular and profitable clients.

Gary admits that too often he takes on work that he does not enjoy just because he has spare time and sometimes he does "freebies" in the hope of winning more business off the back of them. They normally turn out to be a waste of time and sometimes he does not even get his expenses paid for. Gary is a self confessed geek and is always researching what is new in the world of sound and audio visual.

Gary defined his target audience as **event organisers** and his Customer Archetypes break down into:

- The first timers
- The budgeters
- The professionals
- The control freaks
- The scroungers

All of the buyers want sound equipment and/or a sound engineer. That is taken as a given. The primary buying motivation reflects what they are looking for from Gary.

THE FIRST-TIMERS

The primary buying motivation for this group is confidence. They have an event to organise and have not done anything on such a scale before. They could be a PA or a marketing executive. It is a very important event and they want to make sure nothing at all goes wrong. They are unfamiliar with sound equipment and are looking for someone to provide advice and guidance and some 'hand holding'. They are prepared to pay a little more for the assurance that everything will run smoothly.

THE BUDGETERS

The primary buying motivation for this group is cost. They have a budget for the event but it is limited. They want to get the best event possible for their limited budget. They will say something like "What can you do for me for £x?" They are typically charities or local councils. Gary is happy working with these in quieter months because he will still make money but the margins are much lower.

THE PROFESSIONALS

The primary buying motivation for this group is professionalism. These are professional organisers who are in the business of running large scale events for large organisations. Quite often it is an in-house event organiser but equally it could be a private company that organises events for many clients. These people want to work with other professionals who know what they are doing and have good attention to detail. They want their sound engineer to work as part of a team and ideally manage the whole of the audio visual element of the event with very little or no direction. The professionals are usually looking for ideas for something new and fresh to add sparkle to their event.

THE CONTROL FREAKS

The primary buying motivation of this group is expertise. They want the feeling of being in control and seek people who know what they are doing. They think they understand all there is to know about sound and do not welcome suggestions. They tell my client what to do, and when to do it. Gary does not enjoy working with this type of client and they normally find him too expensive anyway.

THE SCROUNGERS

The primary buying motivation of this group is to get something for nothing. They actually have no intention of buying. They give promises of referrals and lots of work in the future if only Gary would help them out this once. They never follow through on their promises and often do not even pay his travel expenses.

Evaluation

Once we had completed the exercise we started to evaluate which of his Customer Archetypes were his ideal clients.

ARCHETYPE	PRIMARY BUYING MOTIVATION	ATTRACTIVENESS
First Timers	Confidence	Medium
Budgeters	Cost	Medium
Professionals	Professionalism	High
Control freaks	Expertise	Low
Scroungers	Free	Low

Gary's "Clients from Hell" were the control freaks and he did not feel like he was ever adding much value. They did not value his input and normally quibbled at his fees.

He decided he would not work with scroungers again unless the event was some kind of charity event.

He quite liked working with the first timers but found that he had to spend a lot of extra time reassuring and educating the event organiser. They were normally one-off events and so less scope for ongoing income.

He liked working with the budgeters as he still made money and they normally just wanted equipment rather than his time. He just did not want to focus on them specifically in terms of sales-lead generation.

The professionals are the group Gary decided to focus his networking and other lead generation efforts on. They were a joy to work with and they really valued his professionalism and innovation.

In articulating his target audience Gary now talks in terms of *professional* event organisers. It is a subtle but important difference that provides greater clarity and will feed into the other aspects of the **APPEAL** framework in subsequent chapters.

Exercise

Now it's your turn to identify your own Customer Archetypes. I hope you get the idea by now. When looking at your existing clients be sure to look at the buying motivation in relation to the specific product or service you are seeking to sell. Look back to an archetype's primary motivation immediately before buying that specific product or service.

ARCHETYPE	PRIMARY BUYING MOTIVATION	ATTRACTIVENESS

Now go through and evaluate your Customer Archetypes in terms of attractiveness and test them by assigning client names to them.

Summary

Defining your Customer Archetypes will enable you to better understand your ideal clients. They are the starting point of the **APPEAL** framework from which all other aspects should flow. To create your Customer Archetypes simply group your existing clients, previous clients and prospects by their primary buying motivation. Then evaluate each of them to identify which Customer Archetype you most want to attract.

five

NO PAIN, NO GAIN

Once David had been through the Customer Archetypes exercise he was visibly more relaxed. He was also getting excited that he could now put his finger on his ideal client and their primary buying motivation. But then he frowned as he realised that he still did not know how he was going to get them interested in talking to him about his IT Solutions.

Introduction

The second part of the **APPEAL** framework is *Pain* and is about better understanding your Customer Archetype's motivation to buy. An important skill in sales is to be able to see things from the perspective of our prospects and clients and that is exactly what we will be doing in this chapter. By the end of the chapter you will have learnt a number of alternative techniques for gaining perspective and have explored the pain of your chosen Customer Archetype.

The Need For Perspective

I work with a lot of people who are stuck in terms of generating sales-leads for their products and services. One of the quickest ways to start getting answers is to see things from the perspective of your target audience. Typical questions I am asked by people looking for answers include:

- How can I generate more sales-leads?
- How can I get more people to pass me referrals?
- How can I increase my prices without losing my client?

The problem is in the question being asked. Each of these questions is seeking to find out HOW? In order to answer their questions I need to ask them two important questions:

WHO specifically are you referring to?

and

WHY specifically...

- would they want to buy your products and services?
- would they want to pass you referrals?
- would they want to continue doing business with you even if you increase your prices?

So far we have addressed the WHO? question by defining your Customer Archetypes. The process broke them down into groups based on primary buying motivation. The buying motivation gives us clues as to why they might become interested but we probably need to do a little more work on seeing things from their perspective.

THE OTHER SIDE OF THE STORY

One way to gain perspective from a client's point of view is by reviewing some of our success stories and zoom in on some of the problems clients were experiencing before we started working with them.

If I were to ask you about one of your best clients and what you did for them I am sure you would wax lyrical about all the great things you did and how they benefited from your products and services. It is perfectly natural to do so. Yet in lead generation terms we would miss out the most important information. What really matters is why they started speaking to you in the first place. By looking at several client success stories for a particular Customer Archetype then we will begin to notice a trend.

I will give a personal example which relates to some work I did a while ago with an IT Value Added Reseller (VAR) who engaged me to help them train their sales people in selling more consulting services. I will present the story in the classic case study format of Problem/Action/Result.

PROBLEM

The problem was that their sales team were excellent at selling products but for some reason they were not selling many add-on services. Sales of services were only a fraction of what they should have been and despite the directors of the company making a big thing about selling services nothing was happening. Margin on product sales were getting smaller and as a result the company was becoming less and less profitable even though their sales were growing at a rate of 40% per year.

ACTION

I worked with the directors, sales managers and the service product manager to diagnose where the problem was. I ran a series of three tailored workshops over a three month period that focused on role play around consultative selling. The workshops were designed to minimise disruption to the sales function. The programme also included a series of group coaching sessions with the sales managers and consulting sessions with the service product manager. These were to address various supplementary issues such as how the sales people were targeted, how the sales people were coached, and how they were educated in the service products.

RESULT

Over a three month period there was a significant improvement in the sale of add-on services. After the very first workshop one sales person used one of the techniques and converted a simple price enquiry for an inexpensive product into a service sale that paid for the complete training and coaching programme.

The format of Problem/Action/Result is a valid approach to creating case studies. Having worked with a number of IT VARS I know that the problem this client was experiencing is a common one. In order to get a sales message that has a lot more bite I need to understand the pain behind their buying motivation. They were initially looking for a sales training course but their primary buying motivation was to change the behaviour of their sales team.

THE STORY BEHIND THE STORY

The information I gave above was typical of the story given when people talk about the work they have done for clients. They say something about what the client wanted, what was delivered and the impact achieved. Have you ever watched some of the movie extras that come with a DVD these days? You often have the directors comments and sometimes a 'behind the scenes' guide as to how the movie was made. That is the story behind the movie.

In the above opportunity I knew what the real story was because I took the opportunity to find it out as part of my sales process. I discovered that this was not the first sales training that had been bought to try and solve the problem. In fact I was number three. They were seeking to turn the company into a solutions focused business but despite all their attempts the sales people did not seem to want to sell services. The company were seemingly doing the right things but not making any progress. The directors and sales managers were feeling frustrated and impatient to say the least.

At first they were a little taken aback when I said that they would probably be wasting their money by just running another sales training course on its own. Once I explained that they needed to approach this in terms of change management rather than sales training I could see the lights coming on. They began to sit up and the ideas started to flow. They began to become more open to looking at their problem differently. My proposal was ten times the cost of what they had intended and what my competitors had proposed. Resolving the problem would be worth a lot of money to them and they had confidence that they would be successful.

In reviewing the story behind the story I get a few key insights as to why they chose me. I have a Customer Archetype I call "The Stuck" and these are people who want to sell more services and despite all their efforts they do not seem to be able to find the answer. If they were just looking for ordinary sales training I would probably not win. I do not fit the classic sales stereotype and my prices are above average. I won the work because I was the only one they spoke to that talked in terms of behaviour change. They also liked the fact that I provided a plan that featured their management at the centre of the change process. In fact my training sessions were probably the least important to the whole change process. Their sales people knew what to do. They had already been trained twice before with little effect! It was more a case of motivating them to put their skills into practice.

When I go through a similar process of examining other success stories I notice a trend emerging as to why my clients choose me. The common theme is that they want change and have not managed to achieve that change through conventional sales training. My NLP (NeuroLinguistic Programming) skills and track record gives them the confidence that I can help them get to the bottom of their problems. When it comes to sales messages around sales training the change element needs to be central.

Exercise

Pick one or more examples of customer success stories with your ideal Customer Archetype. If you do not have any then refer back to the previous chapter where I presented some ideas of how to source examples.

Write out the example in terms of Problem / Action / Result (if you have not already done so) and then write out the story behind the story. Identify why they chose you instead of your competitors. If you do not know then you can always go back and ask!

Feeling The Pain

Whenever I am working with a client on their sales messaging, I find that the story behind the story reveals so much and I start to see points of differentiation emerge that have previously eluded the client. Despite the process being very revealing it is just based on our theorising and feedback from our clients. Clients do not always tell you the whole story. They will probably not tell you how they were really feeling.

I know that many of the smaller businesses I work with are probably going through some severe financial challenges. They will normally be very business-like but I expect some of them, deep down are worried about where their salary cheque is going to come from and how they are going to pay the mortgage. They do not tell me that just like your clients will not always tell you everything that is on their mind. It is possible, however, to take an educated guess using an incredibly powerful and insightful technique I learnt from my NLP training.

The technique is something good sales people and other good communicators often do naturally without even consciously thinking about it. It is to attempt to see things from the other person's perspective. Rather than just theorise like I have done in the story above, this technique is about imagining what it is like to actually be the other person. There is an old Native American Indian saying that you never know what it is like to be someone else until you have travelled a mile in their moccasins. The technique I am about to share with you enables you to attempt to do just that. Mastering this technique, for me, has had a significant impact on my ability to craft compelling sales messages not just for myself but also for clients.

The technique is called *Perceptual Positions*. There are three basic perceptual positions which are actually part of our common daily language.

FIRST POSITION

The first position is how we perceive ourselves. In writing we talk in the first person when we write about our own experiences and thoughts. In our daily activities we are generally in first position. We are thinking about ourselves and the language is "I" and "You". People we speak to are almost certainly in first position and are also saying "I" and "You" too.

SECOND POSITION

When we write in the second person it is as if we take on the thoughts and feelings of another person. Actors playing a part are in the second person living the role as if it was really them. It's like adopting another persona. This is exactly how it is in second position. We imagine we are the other person with their beliefs and world view. We see the world through their eyes. When in second position our language is still "I" and "You". Unlike first position this is done from the other person's perspective. If you are saying:

"If I were them I would be feeling…" then you are not in second position. If you were, then the language would be more like:

"I am feeling…" Then you are along the right lines.

THIRD POSITION

The third person, in writing, is where we are referring to other people. We are commenting on what they have done and giving our opinions about it. The third position is the same idea. It is as if we are seeing things as a neutral bystander. It's what I call the "Fly on the wall" position. The language is very much "He", "She" or "They".

If we feel emotions about the situation then we are not in third position.

For example, let's imagine that we are currently in dispute with someone. First position would tell us how we see things and feel about it. Second position will reveal how the other party sees things and feels about it. Third position will take the emotion out of the situation and see things from a totally neutral perspective.

The technique allows us to gain additional perspectives. People who are highly experienced in this technique can switch between perceptual positions and back in a blink of an eye. For sales messaging, the perceptual position we are particularly interested in is second position and the following is how I teach it to beginners on my public Master-class.

STARS IN THEIR EYES

There is a TV show called *Stars In Their Eyes* where the contestants dress up as a well known singer and impersonate the musical artist. Likewise, in the perceptual positions exercise the attendee sits in the "hot" chair and for five minutes they have to impersonate their target Customer Archetype. They have a partner who has to ask them questions about their problems. The objective of the questioner is to really focus on the problem areas. How is it affecting them personally? How do they feel about it? I encourage the questioner to keep asking deeper and deeper questions until they get words that describe pain. These words are then used later on when we start crafting our success stories.

Exercise

If you have a partner, take it in turns to go through the *Stars In Your Eyes* exercise for your Customer Archetype.

If you do not have a partner then you can do this on your own with two chairs opposite each other. One chair is the "hot seat" and the other for an imaginary person you will be talking to. Put a voice recorder on the floor between the two chairs so that you can capture the exercise.

Firstly sit in the first position chair and start talking about the situation with your client prior to starting to work with them. Next move over to the second position chair and start talking about the situation as if you were your client. The insights may not be totally there to begin with but if you keep talking they will soon come.

Customer Hats

A more sophisticated version of the *Stars In Their Eyes* approach, and the technique I actually use, is what I call "Customer Hats". It was inspired by Edward De Bono's excellent work *Six Thinking Hats*. With De Bono's Thinking Hats system you have different coloured hats for different perspectives. There is one for thinking creatively, another for thinking positively, another for thinking negatively. The idea is that you imagine that you are wearing a particular coloured hat and whilst you are doing so you think from that particular perspective.

So, for example, when I am wearing the Black Hat all my thinking is from the perspective of the negative and I am examining what can go wrong. When I wear the Yellow Hat all my thinking is from a positive and optimistic perspective. I am thinking what could go right and having positive thoughts. The result is that by the time you have gone through all six hats you will have seen things from many different perspectives.

The Customer Hats work by helping you see things from the perspective of your clients. You create an imaginary hat (or even a physical one) to represent each Customer Archetype. You then imagine yourself putting that hat on and wearing it. Whilst you have that hat on you have to talk about things as if you were that type of client. If you have a more complex sale where there are different stakeholders involved then you can create a hat for each different stakeholder. So you may have one for the Finance Director, one for the CEO and so on.

Exercise

Decide what type of hat most represents your Customer Archetype, and go through the *Stars In Their Eyes* exercise again; but this time with the appropriate Customer Hat on.

Case Study

We return to Gary the sound engineer who has decided that his target audience is professional event organisers and his ideal Customer Archetype is "the professionals". He picks a customer success story and puts on his imaginary customer hat and comes up with something like this.

"I have a really prestigious event coming up. We have been running it for the last five years and my client is thinking the event is getting a little tired and wants to freshen it up in some way. My client has given me the idea of using audience voting systems like on *Who Wants To Be A Millionaire?* I have looked at them before but they are a little risky unless done properly. All the people I have seen so far either charge an absolute fortune or we would not be happy to rely on them. We need a safe pair of hands. It's better for us to play it safe than risk a disaster – there is too much at stake."

This exercise reveals to Gary that this Customer Archetype does not like to take risks and wants a "safe pair of hands". The emotional drivers behind the buying motivation are confidence and peace of mind. The accounts are just too important to risk mistakes. Having a safe pair of hands who is also up to date with the latest technology is a fantastic combination.

Gary can see that the audience voting systems he has just invested in could be a very interesting conversation starter when talking to his target audience – but at the end of the day he has to emphasise the fact that he is a "safe pair of hands".

Summary

It is much easier to find the answers in terms of sales-lead generation when we start to see things from our client's perspective. We want to get a better understanding of the emotional drivers impacting the primary buying motivation. There are a number of techniques to help discover this. These are:

- Looking at the story behind the story
- Stars In Their Eyes
- Customer Hats

six

DITCH THE PITCH!

David now had a much better insight into who his ideal clients are and why they might be interested in talking to him. What he was still unable to do was communicate this information in a way that others could understand. I joked with David at how long his introduction was when we first met. He looked at me with disbelief when I told him we were going to summarise it into fifteen words or less.

"Good luck with that one!" he smiled. Unfortunately he declined my invitation to place a bet on it!

Introduction

Whenever people meet each other for the first time, especially at networking meetings, there is one question that is almost guaranteed to come up. The answer you give to this question is very important in terms of how you are thought of and remembered. It is the "What do you do?" question. It has several variants such as:

- What line of business are you in?
- What do you do for a living?
- What kind of work do you do?

Whether you are at a networking meeting, at a party, or speaking to someone in a queue, it is a golden opportunity from a sales-lead generation point of view. That very person could be an ideal client or know someone who is. What you say in response to the "what do you do?" question can have a big impact on what happens next.

The third aspect of the **APPEAL** framework is *Proposition* and in this chapter we will help you to articulate your proposition in fifteen words or less and create your networking introduction.

I will also cover in detail the need for specialization which addresses the fifth aspect of the **APPEAL** framework which is *Advantage*.

Why Pitching Is Ineffective

The quickest way to turn off someone you know, let alone someone you have just met for the very first time, is to subject them to a sales pitch. Whether it is an overt pitch or a cleverly disguised one does not really matter. If your intent is to pitch then that is how it will be perceived by the other person. You may get lucky but you risk spoiling your chances of that person becoming an introducer or even a customer.

There is a time and place for everything and pitching is an important part of the sales process. It is just not effective when you do not know who you are even speaking to. When you go to a networking meeting, do you go to buy? Or do you go to expand your network and find potential clients? You would be safe to assume that most people who attend networking meetings are not there in buying mode. Make it your aim to be remembered for what you do and not for being a pushy sales person.

The Elevator Pitch

Is it any wonder that so many people pitch at networking meetings? We are told by "business experts" that we should have a carefully honed "elevator pitch". They are not necessarily wrong. It is just that the name suggests that you should be overtly selling as opposed to generating interest.

The idea comes from the notion that if you were in a lift with a potential client and they asked you the question "What do you do?" you would be able to pitch your business in the time it takes to travel up a couple of floors. I don't know about you but that has never happened to me! I have met plenty of potential clients at events and I know I have about a minute to start a conversation and gain their interest and a commitment to talk later. That is plenty of time to deliver a fifteen word proposition statement and tell an example story.

I believe the real sentiment behind the elevator pitch as being prepared to make what you do sound attractive to your ideal audience in a very short space of time. The problem with the term 'elevator pitch' is the word "pitch" which is a term normally used in sales to mean making a sales proposal. When you meet a total stranger you have no idea what their needs and wants are. You end up in the "spray and pray" sales syndrome where you pitch to everyone and annoy most people.

Occasionally you will get lucky and if you do enough of it you will achieve some sales success.

The sales process will, however, be much harder as you will be treated like any other pushy sales person. You will be kept at arm's length and prospects will assume that you say or do anything to win the sale. The best sales people I have ever met do not come across as being pushy at all. They know that when a prospect believes that you might be able to relieve their pain then the dynamic of the relationship totally changes. They are far more open and forthcoming with information. You will also be more trusted which goes a long way, especially if you are selling your own services where trust is so important.

Let's say you are at a family wedding and a guest asks you:

"What do you do?"

Would you launch into a fully blown sales pitch? I am sure you would not be that popular if you did. With the softer approach that I am going to show you later in the chapter you will seize the opportunity to stimulate a discussion about your products and services. It will also be conducive to good relationships. You will get the benefits of the 'elevator pitch' without the negative consequences.

Introduction Styles

Here are some of the most common styles of introduction I come across at networking meetings:

- The sales pitch
- The long ramble
- The Clever Trevor
- The laundry list
- The story
- The plain and simple

THE SALES PITCH

With this type of introduction you are left in no doubt that the person making the introduction is selling directly to you. You see it a lot at networking meetings such as speed networking and events where you have a minute to introduce yourself. People who go to these events are normally looking to develop new clients for themselves and just switch off when they are being pitched at. Then they proceed to do a pitch themselves whilst everyone else switches off!

I met up for a one-on-one meeting one morning with a lady I had previously encountered at a breakfast networking meeting. She had pitched her accounting services to the room suggesting that everyone needs to use her services. It turned out that she specialised in working with much more established companies and no one in the room would have been suitable anyway. The sales pitch was letting her down in two respects:

Firstly people's perceptions of her will have been shaped by her pitch. She was being perceived as a pushy person who dealt with very small businesses when the truth was the opposite. Secondly, people in the room would be less likely to want to spend time with her and potentially introduce her to their clients because the assumption is that she would be pushy with them too. In reality she was not pushy at all. She was just doing what she thought was normal and actually she felt very uncomfortable about it

If someone is pushy with you then it is reasonable to assume that they will be pushy with anyone you introduce them to. Would you recommend someone like that to your closest and most trusted contacts?

We want to stimulate a discussion of your products and services – without turning people off – and increase your chances of the other person being willing to help you get connected with people that need what you have to offer. The sales pitch leaves a lot to be desired in this respect.

THE LONG RAMBLE

This style of introduction is where the person rambles on incoherently about something or other. It is a favourite amongst technically minded people. After a minute or two people listening are in total confusion. The reaction will be polite and people will pretend to be listening whilst secretly thinking about what they are going to have for dinner that evening or an important phone call they need to make!

THE CLEVER TREVOR

This is where the person uses some kind of clever metaphor to try and describe what they do. For example, I met someone once who, when I asked him what he did I got the reply:

"I am a pilot and I help people sail through uncharted waters". It turned out that he was a coach! For a moment I thought he really was a pilot and was starting to ask him questions about what kind of boats he sailed!

If done well and given some context this type of introduction will invoke a response like:

"What is that exactly?"

If my friend had prefixed his introduction with:

"I am a life coach," – for example, "I am a life coach and my clients see me as a pilot helping them sail through uncharted waters," then I would not have been so confused. Before starting my business I attended a coaching course where they were teaching this kind of introduction. It does not surprise me that so many coaches struggle to earn a living if this is what they are being taught!

THE LAUNDRY LIST

This is where the person answers the question "What do you do?" quite literally. They reel off a number of different things, such as:

"I run a nursery playgroup, I am also a distributor for a cosmetics firm, I can do colour analysis, and I am a trained life coach". I believe the sentiment behind the laundry list is that if one provides enough options then someone may latch onto one. I can understand this line of thought. The trouble is that people could quite easily get the impression that you are a Jack of all trades, and master of none. Secondly, in my experience, people tend to have a limited capacity to remember.

It's much better to focus on one area where you most want to generate leads from your networking and be remembered. This woman could, perhaps, focus solely on the nursery group in the knowledge that she sells lots of cosmetics and colour analysis to the parents and is now starting to successfully offer life coaching to her cosmetics clients.

THE STORY

I have been a member of many breakfast meeting organisations like BNI, 4 Networking, NRG Networks and others. The thing I noticed early on was that the people that seemed to do the best would tell a story of what they had been doing recently for their clients. There were many different variations of this style and in the next chapter I will be proposing a story format that has helped many people who were already using the story approach to get even better results.

The important thing is that stories help to get the message across in an enjoyable and low pressured way. It's amazing how they help listeners to think of people they know similar to the person in the story.

THE PLAIN AND SIMPLE

Typically people using this approach will introduce themselves in ways such as, "I am a printer" or "I work for a printing company". The introduction is short and natural. The only trouble is that it does not really say very much about what you do and who you do it for. The other person is left making assumptions of what a printer does. The person could specialise in a specific area of printing such as very large print sizes. Saying he works as a printer specialising in very large print sizes would probably yield so much better results.

Recommendation

My recommendation is to use an advanced version of the *plain and simple* approach followed immediately by an example story. They can each be used individually, but when they are used together they are incredibly effective. For the remainder of this chapter we will be focusing on your *plain and simple* statement, also known as your proposition statement, where we will summarise what you do in just fifteen words or less. In the next chapter we will build your example stories to amplify your *plain and simple* statement.

Box Theory

I have a theory which I call "Box Theory". Whether it is true or not is actually irrelevant because if you act as if it were true you will get fantastic results! The purpose of Box Theory is to get people to take charge over how they are remembered by others when they network.

Box Theory states that when you meet someone for the first time they want to put you into a box within their memory. We all have metaphorical boxes in our minds and one way in which we remember others is to think of them in terms of their occupation. We put them into a box. So when people ask you what you do, be clear that they are preparing to put you in a suitable box within their memory.

Some people try and avoid being put into a box. They are, however, fighting human nature which is always futile in my experience. It's like trying to swim against the tide. I remember meeting a PR consultant for a one-on-one conversation. He was talking about all the weird and wacky work that he had done for companies. I asked him about his target audience and he got very defensive and said that he did not want to be put into a box. He went straight into my "weird and wacky" box!

People will put you in a box whether you like it or not. Rather than resist the inevitable, I recommend you proactively make it clear to people which box they should put you in. The choice is clear: choose your box or leave it to chance. Unless you do something very unusual then choosing your own box will increase your results from networking significantly.

Why Box Theory Matters

When you network extensively then you will meet a lot of people, many of whom will also network with others extensively. People who network properly will tend to come across opportunities. When this happens then the natural reaction is to think; "who do I know that might be suitable?"

You want to be the one remembered if a suitable opportunity comes up. The trouble is that there may be plenty of other perfectly nice and equally talented people in the same box as you. Your chance of being remembered increases significantly if you put yourself in a specialist box of your own. The other thing is that when people make recommendations or they use a supplier then they will often play it safe. Would you rather choose a generalist or a specialist to help you solve an important problem?

I used to sell into the travel industry and there was a strong preference for using people who specialise in the travel industry. If a person is having problems sleeping and is seeking a coach, do you think that person would prefer to work with someone who was a generalist coach or someone who specialises in coaching people through their sleep problems?

Specialise Rather Than Generalise

I can understand why some people resist specialising. There are a lot of things they can do and they do not want to restrict it. I met someone like that one day whilst at a networking lunch run by NRG Networks. After some small talk I asked him what he did. He said he was a lawyer. There are a lot of lawyers who attend meetings like this one. I asked if he specialised in any particular area of law to which he replied enthusiastically:

"Yes, I specialise in construction."

"That's interesting," I replied, "what does that involve?" He went on to tell me how the construction industry is notorious for disputes between builders, clients, and architects. He helps to prevent those disputes from happening in the first place or resolving them when they do. Immediately I thought of three architects that I know well I could possibly introduce him to. I asked him why he did not say that he specialised in construction to which he replied:

"Well we do so much more than that." He then went on to confess that he had yet to generate any business from networking in well over a year.

It's a little like the story of the monkey who gets his hand stuck in the goody jar because it is trying to grab everything and its hand gets too full to withdraw. If it were to just take one at a time it could quickly empty the jar. Instead the monkey ends up with nothing. Once I understood which box to place this lawyer in it was much easier to understand how I could help him.

When a potential client thinks about why they should choose you, then the fact that you are a specialist in that area will give you a competitive advantage and make the sale so much easier. It is a paradox in that when we take the leap of faith and let go of trying to win everything we end up selling a great deal more.

Specialise Rather Than Summarise

I come across a lot of people who do a wide number of things and find it hard work to articulate a common theme. For example, we had the lady running a nursery playgroup, plus distributing cosmetics, providing colour analysis, and also life coaching. Often when people are working on the "What do you do?" question they try and summarise. They seek something common in everything they do. What is the common factor between all these things for this lady? They end up going round and round in circles and finish up with some kind of "Clever Trevor" type of networking introduction.

What I helped this lady to do was to focus on her nursery school and define an area of specialisation for the school.

I rarely find that summarising is the right way to go. Normally the answer is in specialising in one aspect where the individual has maximum credibility and plenty of success stories. I look for something a little different and evidence that it is solving a real problem that people are prepared to spend good money on. It's about finding the best box for them.

A good example of the power of specialising is an IT Consultant called Jamie with whom I worked some time ago. He did a lot of networking and had a reputation as being a nice person to meet. His introduction style was the "long ramble" and as a result he was not getting any significant business coming from his networking activities. We looked at where he had the biggest amount of credibility and skills and that turned out to be in the area of SMS technology. That is text messaging to you and me. Something he forgot to tell people.

We decided that in terms of Box Theory he would be in the text messaging box and that he should seek alliances with web designers and those likely to be considering working with text messaging technology. We started to build some success stories around the work he had done for clients in the area of text messaging. He proceeded to contact all the web designers he knew and I spoke to all the web designers I knew at the time. Almost immediately he started finding potential projects and his business started growing very quickly. The growth mostly came through people he already knew. They previously had no idea how to help him because he was far too generalised and they did not understand his technical jargon.

Specialising In Everything

I have come across some people who latch onto the power of the word "specialise" and then ruin it by doing a "laundry list" introduction. In the example of the lawyer above it would go something like:

"I work for X,Y, and Z Solicitors and we specialise in Construction, Litigation, Family Law, Corporate Law and most other areas of law."

This is an exaggeration of what people do, but when you say that you specialise in several things you effectively say you are a generalist. I believe that people are far too intelligent to fall for something like that! What we need to do is emphasise the area where you feel most capable of generating sales-leads and for which you have credible examples of success.

Specialising does not mean you no longer stop offering other products and services. When training people in Box Theory I use an analogy of a car boot sale and two traders having a stall next to each other. Both have a pasting table covered with items for sale and at first glance there is no difference between the two tables. They both have a few glasses, a few unwanted books, and selected pieces of crockery. It is likely though that there are one or two items on one table that are different to the other.

If the traders were to emphasis these items of difference they are more likely to attract the attention of people looking for these items. Once they have their attention then it becomes so much easier to sell them the other things on the table where there is much less differentiation. In the same way see specialisation as a way of winning a new client and then once you have delivered in your area of specialisation they will be more likely to buy your other products and services which are less differentiated from your competitors.

Creating Your Introduction

There are lots of different ways in which you can put together your introduction. This is why I have taken the time to explain the underlying psychology for you. The reality is that people are unlikely to remember much. The more you say the less they will remember. Unfortunately our brains seem to be hard-wired to take limited input, which is why the word specialise helps to retain the focus of attention.

I am going to give you a template for starting to construct more impactful introduction statements. Most people start with the template and very quickly start to get better results. After a while they go on to fine tune it. Let's begin with the key elements so we can start developing your introduction.

There are two parts to the introduction:

1. The Prefix – eg "I work as a………."
2. The Proposition statement – "I specialise in…….."

I aim to get the proposition statement down to fifteen words or less. The prefix should be short too. People's ability to retain information is limited and they will probably only remember a few key words. The more words you put into your introduction the less likely that people listening will remember anything. Less is more.

Stories are much easier to remember and they will do most of the work in generating sales-leads. The proposition statement is specifically to enable you to be remembered for your target audience and area of specialisation.

A Template For Putting Your Introduction Together

- **\<Prefix\>** followed by...
- I specialise in helping **\<target audience\>** to **\<what you do for them\>**

The word "helping" can be substituted for another word such as enabling, providing, etc.

EXAMPLE 1

- **Prefix:** I am a tax accountant and
- **Statement:** I specialise in helping self-employed people pay less tax and avoid fines.

Here we have a professional who has a very personal approach. His target audience is self-employed people and what he does for them is help them pay less tax and avoid fines.

EXAMPLE 2

- **Prefix:** I run an IT consultancy and
- **Statement:** We specialise in enabling IT directors to turn around failing projects.

Here we have someone who wants to be seen as the CEO of a more established business. In his statement he begins with "We" rather than "I". His target audience is IT Directors. What he does for them is enable them to turn around failing IT projects.

EXAMPLE 3

- **Prefix:** I work for a large IT software company and
- **Statement:** We specialise in enabling retailers to accurately predict the buying behaviour of their customers.

In this one we have someone who is working as an account manager for a well known company. We could have extended the prefix to include lots more but it would have meant less attention to the statement. Fortunately he was more interested in sales-leads than letting everyone know who he worked for or his job title.

The important information here is the inclusion of his target audience – retailers – and what he does for them.

Previously he was talking about Business Intelligence software and then having to go into a long winded explanation about what Business Intelligence is. What matters is that his clients are retailers wanting to understand customer behaviour.

Case Study

Back to Gary and his sound engineering business. Gary developed his introduction as:

I am a sound engineer and I specialise in helping professional event organisers run their major events.

Let's break it down:

- **<Prefix>** - I am a sound engineer
- **<Target Audience>** - Professional event organisers
- **<What you do for them>** - run their major events

What people will associate with Gary are the following key words: Sound engineer, professional event organisers, major events.

Gary's networking introduction now gets him remembered by people he meets and his existing network in the way he wants. When combined with a short example story it brings his proposition statement to life. When he tells them both in combination he finds that people not only remember him but also recall event organisers they know.

Exercise

Now is the time for you to work on your introduction. Use the template above and when doing it consider the insights you have gained about your target audience, their buying motivation and what they are really buying. Maybe do several versions and get people in your network to give you feedback on which best resonates with them. Remember to specialise based on your area of maximum credibility.

Summary

Keeping your introduction simple and specific will greatly increase your chances of being remembered for what you do. We looked at box theory and how we need to take charge of how people remember us rather than leaving it to chance. We finished by looking at a template for re-working your networking introduction.

seven

CRAFTING YOUR EXAMPLE STORIES

David was very pleased with his proposition statement. It was short and to the point. David turned to me and asked:

"How is this going to generate any sales-leads?" He had heard so much about elevator pitches that he felt the proposition statement was not very "salesy". I laughed and explained that the fact that it did not come across as a sales pitch was what made it so powerful and that the stories do all the selling.

"I am not very good at telling stories," said David "I can't tell a joke to save my life!" I reassured him that he did not have to be a good storyteller at all as long as the story followed the right structure.

Introduction

The fourth element of the **APPEAL** Framework is *Example* and this relates to example stories which we are going to cover in this chapter. We will create your stories that you will be able to tell in less than a minute.

So that you can learn the various key elements of a story we are going to develop your stories in stages. It is the same process that I use on my master class to enable me to get people to a high level of competence in less than an hour. The stories are best spoken rather than written. If you can, find a partner to work through the exercises with. Perhaps your partner can work on their stories at the same time. Alternatively, you could write out the stories or just speak out aloud to an imaginary person, a chair, or even a teddy bear! Do it in a relaxed way as if you were standing by a water cooler or coffee machine.

Example Of An Introduction And Story Together

I am at a networking meeting talking to someone called John and I have discovered that he has an IT consulting business. He has attended the meeting because he wants to generate more local business. I have not said anything about what I do, having focused my attention and interest solely on him.

John: So Richard, What do you do?

Me: I work as a sales consultant and I specialise in enabling IT companies sell more consulting services.

John: So how does that work? (I can see from his face that his interest has been heightened)

Me: Well, perhaps if I give you an example...

I have recently been working with the owner of a business specialising in database management. She had done some brilliant work for one client and was struggling to get other companies interested even though they stood to save a lot of money. She was really worried that she was too dependent on one large client and was desperate to win a couple more clients. I was introduced as a specialist in sales messaging and we spent a half a day working on her proposition and lead generation strategy. She now has a healthy sales pipeline and is expecting to close her first sale shortly.

John: Blimey! How did you do that?

Me: Well they did all the work. In fact they were doing almost everything right. I just helped them to find that missing piece of the jigsaw. I would be happy to meet over coffee sometime and better understand what you do.

John then hands me his card and I agree to call. At this stage I do not know if John is a potential introducer or a potential client or even both!

Some people would have launched straight into a sales pitch. I take a consultative approach. I would much rather get a proper one-on-one meeting with John where he feels more comfortable in opening up and discussing his issues. My ultimate goal is to be seen as a trusted advisor and in my experience that should start at the very first meeting. It is not about giving away free consultancy. It's about being seen as someone who can be trusted and someone safe to be recommended.

Getting Started

I would like to start you off by getting you to just tell a story, no matter how good or bad you think it is. We will then go through a process of refining it and turning it into a lead generation story.

Exercise

Tell the story of what you or your company did for one of your ideal clients. This should be one that is a good example to support the area of specialisation you previously identified.

Stories Are About People

When people typically have their first go at telling their customer story they talk about an organisation unless they sell directly to the general public. They also normally talk about what they did for the organisation. I would like you to assume that your prospects or clients are not really interested in you and what you did. If they can relate to the person in the story then you stand a chance of generating interest especially if they are going through something similar– or know someone else who is.

To be most effective the story should be about someone similar to your ideal Customer Archetype. You do not have to name the person in the story. It works just as well if you refer to the person by their job title. For example:

"We have recently been working for the Finance Director of an international bank and…" or "I am currently working with a business owner of a software company and…"

Stories Should Have Drama

The thing that makes a story really compelling is the drama. On TV the soap operas always seeks what is known as the "cliff hanger". It's a metaphor for the emotional drama. Someone is hanging off the edge of cliff gripping on with his bare hands and we do not know whether he is going to be able to claw his way back up the cliff, be rescued, or whether he will get to the point where he no longer has the strength to hang on. Good drama in books is what gets people to keep reading. People sometimes refer to a good book as a "page turner".

Wherever there is emotion there is drama. The stronger the emotion the more compelling the drama becomes. People feel emotions. Inanimate objects do not. In the movie *Herbie,* the car is given human characteristics and so was able to be the centre of the drama. Companies, products, and services are concepts. If we want a story with drama we need to focus on specific people within the company or specific customers of products and services.

When you tell your example story you want the person listening to relate to the person in the story and their situation, or recall someone they know who is going through a similar experience.

Finding The Drama

Once people start to understand how to emphasise the drama then this storytelling technique becomes much easier for them. I often get technically minded people attending my Master-class and they sometimes initially struggle to see how there is drama behind their client's current situation.

I can remember one such person saying to me:

"'I specialise in supporting email systems. Where is the drama in that?" He gave me an example of a client which generates a lot of online enquiries. When you focus on the system then it is hard to identify the drama. Switch to the people impacted by the email systems and it becomes much easier. It turns out that they were called into the client because the email server kept on crashing. It was approaching the quarter end and the Sales Director was struggling to reach his targets. He was fairly relaxed the first time it happened, but now the Sales Director was shouting down the phone demanding the IT Director do something to sort out the problem. That is the point at which they got the call.

Can you see the drama of the situation? Can you relate to the Sales Director's frustration? Can you imagine the pressure the IT Director must be feeling? The email systems consultant was too focused on the email system. It is not a human and has no emotions. The people being affected by losing all the sales-leads had plenty of emotions!

Another example I remember is a tax accountant who claimed that people found tax boring and there was no drama in getting your tax done. I made up a couple of examples and she admitted that they rang true for several of her clients when she first started working with them.

One of these stories was the scenario of a business owner short of cash and struggling to pay himself a wage. He had been avoiding doing his tax because he was worried he would get a bill he could not pay. He finally started speaking to the tax accountant because he was scared about the letters he had begun to receive threatening severe fines. He reluctantly engaged the tax accountant and very quickly was nicely surprised that she had managed to find several items that ultimately led to a tax rebate. He ended up with enough extra cash to be able to pay himself for the next couple of months.

Can you imagine how it feels to be short of money and worried about not being able to pay for your basic living expenses let alone pay your tax bill? Can you imagine how that business owner now feels? This is the essence of the drama of the story and what makes example stories so powerful.

It's the drama and the emotions in your story that people will relate to. This is what will make them memorable. Not everyone you meet will be going through that drama right now but may do in the future. You also want them to remember you when they meet someone going through a similar drama.

I have this vision of two people sat in the pub on a Friday night. One person is sharing their woes with the other and as they do they remember the story you told them.

"Funny you say that!" they say, "I met someone recently who was telling me how they..." They then proceed to tell your story. It may not be word perfect but they will have the essence of the drama and the happy ending. This is an example of how a good example story can spread.

Exercise

Re-visit your story and ensure the focus is on the person like the one you hope to meet. Emphasise the drama of the situation. Make sure you tap into the emotions that you discovered in chapter five.

The Payoff

Whilst it is important to focus your stories on your clients situation before you started working with them you do need to say something about yourself and what you did for them and what they got from it. The way I explain the balance is to resort to fairy stories. In every good fairy story there is a damsel in distress who is having problems with a dragon. The damsel in distress is your client and the dragon is the problem that is causing the drama. Also in the fairly story is the knight in shining armour who comes along and saves the day. The knight is the hero and that is you. The knight in shining armour is important but the story is not about him. What causes the story to be special is the drama around the damsel in distress and her struggle. The knight saves the day when it seems all hope is lost and makes for a happy ending.

The payoff should be more about the results the client got from working with you. I am often asked why I recommend that the story contains so little about what was done for the client. My response is that if the person you are speaking to wants to know they will ask you. They will say something like "Tell me more!" or "Wow, how did you manage that?" If they are interested in what you have said then it will start a discussion. Sometimes they respond immediately and sometimes they will come back to you later. The great thing is that if they are not interested or they do not relate to the person in the story then it's just a story. By saying in your proposition statement that you are a specialist in this area means that people will assume you know what you are doing.

By taking out the detail of what you did means a typical story need not take more than a minute. In my Master-class I normally give people three minutes to begin with and then we end up getting them to just below a minute. No more than 40% of your story should be about you and the payoff.

Example

I recently worked with a sales trainer who was in a predicament. He was being asked by an existing big client to quote for a series of half day workshops. His client made it clear that there was a lot of competition and he felt that he was expected to lower his rates. He was worried that this would set a trend for all future work and yet, at the same time, he was desperate to win this new project. It would open all sorts of doors for him. *He had heard about my single session sales coaching and called to talk things through.* After thirty minutes he had decided that, given all the facts he would actually increase his rates. A couple of days later he phoned me excitedly saying that he had not only won the project but also the client had put him forward for another even bigger opportunity.

The drama in this example is the decision that he needs to make. Does he lower his rates and risk being locked into lower rates for all future work? Or does he keep the rates the same and risk losing the project? Did you notice the emotive words? "Predicament", "worried", "desperate". Did you notice that I did not even mention anything specific about how I did it? Did you notice the payoff? For those with an eye for detail, did you notice that the story was 152 words long of which only forty-eight relate to the payoff?

Exercise

Now refine your story to add lots of drama and emotive words and a good payoff.

Adding Impact To Your Stories

STIMULATE THE IMAGINATION

A good story causes the listener to imagine the story in their "mind's eye". This is a form of visualisation called mental rehearsal. Athletes use this to see themselves winning a race. The ideal scenario is where an ideal prospect puts themselves into the story and relates personally to it. If your prospect can see themselves working with you then you have made a big step forward towards them becoming a client at some stage.

The more concrete you make your stories the easier it is for other people to imagine them. Adding details like colours, smells, sounds, feelings etc make it much easier to form a mental picture.

Compare the following two sentences:

The man left the restaurant.

The man put on his grey coat and smiled at the waitress as he left the restaurant.

The second contains motion and the visuals of the coat and smiling. Stories still work without these extra flourishes but it will just make them more memorable by sticking in their imagination.

REFERENCES TO TIME

"Once upon a time" is a classic start to a children's story. It acts like a cue to get us ready to listen to stories. It also serves another purpose in transporting the listener's imagination to a different place. Using "Once upon a time" in our stories would lose all credibility. You can get a similar effect by inserting a time reference. You will notice that your day-to-day anecdotes have them and our selling stories should have them too. For example:

"Recently I have been…"

"Last month I did some work for…"

"Only last week I was…"

"We are currently working with..."

It does not need to be specific. In fact in many cases you may want to leave the time reference as vague so that it does not sound too recent or too much in the past.

PUTTING WORDS INTO YOUR CLIENT'S MOUTH

If you were to say something like:

"Our products and services are the best on the market" then your prospects are unlikely to believe you. However, they are more likely to believe it if it is said by the person in the story.

VOICE AND BODY LANGUAGE

If you are with a prospect in person then you have the advantage of being able to fully utilise your voice and body language to reinforce your stories. For example, if you are quoting someone saying something then you may want to change your voice slightly when you imitate their words. You can use your hands to paint out the picture in the air.

TRANSITIONS

In storytelling the transitions are when you go from normal conversation into a story and then back to normal conversation. Examples of transitions into a story include:

"That reminds me of a time when…"

"Did I ever tell you about…"

"It's a bit like when…"

"For example…"

Examples of transitions back to the conversation might include phrases like

"Anyway..."

"I guess what I am saying is..."

"The bottom line is..."

"So..."

People who are highly skilled at storytelling are very good at transitions so you do not really notice when they slip in and out of storytelling mode.

LINKS

Links are very useful to cut out large chunks of the story and get from one place to another. It is literally the link from one part of a story to another. It's a little bit like a transition within the body of the story but it is specific rather than vague. I mentioned above about minimising in the story what you did for the client. This is because until you have established that they have a similar problem they probably do not care. The other thing is that the part about what you did is most likely to end up being the biggest part of the story and add an extra couple of minutes to a one-minute story.

Let's re-look at a story I have used earlier in the chapter. I have highlighted the link sentence for you.

I recently worked with a sales trainer who was in a predicament. He was being asked by an existing big client to quote for a series of half day workshops. His client made it clear that there was a lot of competition and he felt that he was expected to lower his rates. He was worried that this would set a trend for all future work and yet, at the same time, he was desperate to win this new project. It would open all sorts of doors for him. He had heard about my single session sales coaching and called to talk things through. After thirty minutes he had decided that, given all the facts he would actually increase his rates. A couple of days later he phoned me excitedly saying that he had not only won the project but the client had also put him forward for another even bigger opportunity.

We have just a short sentence that explained how I got involved and then it goes straight into the payoff. Other examples of links I commonly use include:

"An existing client recommended me to them and..."

"I was working with them on another project and..."

"They liked the fact that I specialise in working with non-sales people and..."

Links allow you to say a lot with a few words. A client recommending you will say that you are good enough to be recommended. Working with a client on another project says that you are good enough for your clients to re-use you on more than one project. Including the fact that they liked your area of specialisation helps to emphasise your point of difference.

When you apply an understanding of language and perception to your stories you can get across a lot of information in a short space of time. Much of the inferences are subtle and may not get picked up consciously. My experience is that they still have an impact.

WHEN YOU DO NOT HAVE ANY STORIES

I sometimes get asked how to handle a product or service that you have not sold before and so do not have any stories. Ideally you should be focusing winning new clients on an area of specialism rather than something new. Existing clients who know you, like you, and trust you, may be a great source of interest for new products and services where you do not need to work so hard to establish your credibility because you have already done some great work for them.

One technique is the "We are currently talking to" technique. For example:

"We are currently talking to the Operations director of XYZ who..." and then launching into the standard type of story. You will either leave off the payoff altogether or if you want to be open about the fact that it's a new product then you may finish with something like:

"So far..." or "they are expecting to..."

Unless they are already a skilled storyteller they are unlikely to pick up that you have not yet fully implemented the project. For that reason I personally would be very selective as to where you use this technique. There is nothing worse in spending time generating interest only to lose the sale and your credibility further down the line when your prospect wants more details of where you have previously done something similar.

Another approach is to share the stories of colleagues and associates. You will need to ensure you use "we" and not "I" in your stories so it is presented as the collective experience rather than personal experience. I have worked with people who have bought a franchise that have specific processes. In these cases a new franchisee was able to do anything that more established franchisees could do so it did not matter that they borrowed their stories until they had established some of their own.

I would seriously advise against making up a story. Somehow clients always seem to find out and as trust is such a critical part of a long term profitable relationship, deception is not the way to begin it!

Case Study

Here is Gary's introduction followed by his example story:

I am a sound engineer and I specialise in helping professional event organisers run major events

For example...

I have recently been working on a major event for an organiser who was under a lot of pressure from her client to enable the audience to vote using the sort of thing you see on *Who Wants To Be A Millionaire?* She was really worried about this as they can be quite tricky to set-up and lots of things can go wrong. I was introduced to her as an expert and a safe pair of hands. I ended up doing both the sound and the voting. The event was a fantastic success and she is now planning to use me on other events coming up soon.

Can you spot the following?

- The person
- The drama
- The payoff
- The time reference
- The link

Gary developed about six stories to emphasise different things. He managed to get three different stories out of this one assignment. In addition to the voting system project there was also drama around the event organiser having been let down by the previous sound engineer and the drama around the whole thing being done at very short notice.

Summary

Your example stories are the things that generate sales-leads for you over time. Example stories complement your proposition statement. A good story is memorable because of the drama and emotion together with the payoff. There is a simple formula to building up example stories that are less than a minute long.

eight

GENERATING SALES-LEADS FROM YOUR NETWORK

David was now very excited. For the first time since he had set up his business he had, clear in his mind, who his target audience are and why they would be interested in having a sales conversation with him. He had a clear and short description of what he did plus a couple of example stories to support it. Sitting with him, I could see that he was now keen to put what he had learnt into practice...

"Now that I have my proposition statement and stories, how am I going to be able to use them to start winning more business?"

Introduction

Now that you have a clear networking proposition and example stories it is time to start getting the word out and focus on generating interest in your products and services. In this chapter we look at the final aspect of the **APPEAL** framework which is *Links*. We will explore how to leverage the network you already have to assist you in generating sales-leads.

Begin With Your Clients

In working with companies to help generate sales-leads, I normally find that existing clients are often overlooked. Top sales people know that it is easier to sell more to a satisfied client than to find a new one. They also know that satisfied clients are more likely to be willing to make referrals and help you win more business.

One of my first clients was the owner of a web design company who was struggling to find enough work to make ends meet. It turned out that she had not been keeping in touch with her previous clients. I got her to phone five of her most recent clients the next day and out of five companies, three had plans to further develop their website. My client had assumed they would phone her when they needed further work. They had assumed she was not interested as she had not been in touch. Fortunately she was able to rectify the situation but she learnt the lesson!

If you have not spoken to certain clients for a while then make sure you at least call them and ideally agree to meet up for coffee or lunch to get an update from them and to give them some ideas. You should be treating them as part of your network the same as anyone else.

Example stories are really effective when meeting up with existing clients. You can use them to answer the question "What have you been up to lately?" Choosing the right story is a bit of an art form. The more you pay attention to problems that your clients are experiencing, the easier it will be to select the right story and stimulate some interest. Typically they will say something like:

"That sounds very familiar! What did that involve?" Because the example stories are designed to be memorable they can have a delayed effect. I have had many cases where there has been no initial response and yet the story had clearly registered because the client came back at a later date to talk about an issue and referred to the story.

Seeking additional business from your existing clients should also include links into other parts of the same organisation. For example, if your client is a small part of a larger group of companies then you should be seeking to get a recommendation to sister companies or even the parent company. Do your research in terms of the names of the companies and then ask your contact something like:

"Who is your counterpart in XYZ Ltd?"

When they tell you then simply ask for an introduction:

"I would love to talk to them and see if they have similar issues. Would you mind sending them an email introduction and copy me?"

I have never had a request for an email introduction denied. When I used to ask clients to call and speak to their counterpart then it did not always get done. It does not take much effort to send an email, especially if they do not know their counterparts that well. The email means that when you call it will be much easier to get the conversation going than just calling out of the blue. When you meet up then your example stories should be relating to the work done with their colleagues.

When working within large organisations you should aim to build up a mini-network of people within that organisation. You would apply the same principles to this group as to your wider network. It is important to maintain the relationships with these contacts as they could lead to your hearing about potential opportunities both within the organisation and with their external contacts too.

When I was selling IT Consultancy my boss called this 'Walking the corridors' and convinced me that it was the best way to generate sales-leads from existing clients. Walking the corridors is effectively networking within a large organisation. It's about keeping in touch, showing your face whilst looking and listening out for problems you can solve. Sometimes keeping in touch is as simple as putting your head around the door and saying "Hello".

Eating lunch in the staff canteen with client contacts has always been my favourite way of keeping in touch and expanding contacts at the same time. People will often join some of their colleagues and introductions would normally be followed by questions like:

"So what are you doing for us?" and "who else are you working with?" which are perfect cues for an example story or two!

Six Degrees Of Separation

Have you ever heard the term "Six Degrees of Separation"? The idea is that you can connect any two random people in six connections or less. Each person of a certain age knows at least

200 people. People in business who proactively engage in networking will know considerably more. Let's stay with 200 people for simplicity. If everyone you know also knows 200 people, and each of those knows 200 people then you have potentially 40,000 connections. If you go one more degree of separation you go to 8 million people. Six degrees of separation covers sixty-four trillion people which is more people than the entire population of the planet! In the UK alone, three degrees of separation is normally all that is needed.

When you develop a trusted relationship with one of your contacts and they become an advocate then you suddenly duplicate your sales effort. What makes this even more effective is when they directly know and are working with your target audience. Many owners of small businesses or even sole traders may know or have your ideal client on their client list. There becomes a joint benefit of developing a relationship based on trust and advocacy. It can, however, take time to develop such relationships.

This for me is the essence of networking for business. Your network helps you get closer to the people that will help you succeed using the principles of Six Degrees of Separation. It is said that everyone is less than six connections away from the President of the United States. Likewise there is a game where people attempt to establish a connection with actor Kevin Bacon and another actor through their acting roles in less than six connections. If it is possible to connect you with the President of the United States or Kevin Bacon in six connections or less then it must be true that all of your ideal clients are less than six connections away from you. Indeed anyone you meet is connected in some way to people you want to meet or knows someone who is. They may not know people in your target audience personally but they probably know someone who can help you get closer to them.

Building Your Contact List

We need to start to build up a list of names and then prioritise them in terms of making contact and reconnecting. Anyone you already know is connected to you in some way and this is the best place to start.

The method I was taught to develop a list of names is to get a piece of paper or a spreadsheet and write as many headings as you can such as:

- Family
- Friends
- Colleagues at current employer
- Colleagues at previous employer
- Colleagues at other employers
- People from church
- People from school
- People from college
- People from clubs
- Suppliers
- Clients
- Parents of children
- Etc

For each group seek to put down ten or more names. It is important not to pre-judge at this stage. You will probably remember more names by just writing down any that come to mind. Once you have your list then the next step is to prioritise. There will be people on your list that you have no intention of connecting with. You will also not necessarily have time to meet with everyone on the list.

Once your list is completed you need to assess the people on it in terms of the strength of the relationship and how willing they will be to help you.

Exercise

Take ten minutes to create your list. It is worth doing even if you have been networking for a while. We all tend to focus on the people we have had recent contact with and overlook those people who we have had a good connection to in the past but may have lost contact with.

PRIORITISING YOUR LIST

Give each person on your list a score between zero and five in terms of the quality of the relationship. A score of five means that you have a great relationship with them and they are always pleased to see you and help you wherever they can. At the other end of the scale, zero means there is no relationship and no real desire or prospect of building a relationship over time. If you only vaguely know someone but there is no reason to avoid them then give them a score of one. You are still more connected than a total stranger! Zero is really for those who you have no intention of getting back in touch with. Anyone else should have a score of at least one and hopefully many will fall somewhere between two and five.

Once you have gone through the scoring process you can then sort your list by the relationship score with the highest scores on the top and the lowest on the bottom. Leave the zeros from this list.

Getting Reconnected

Online social networking sites Linkedin or Facebook are a fantastic tool for finding and reconnecting to people on your list that you have lost touch with. They are also good for staying in touch and managing your network. Facebook has historically been more friendship focused but is becoming an increasingly important tool for business. LinkedIn has historically been more focused on work-related connections and is becoming more social.

There is a good chance that a lot of people on your list with whom you do not already have regular contact will be on either LinkedIn or Facebook. I recommend that you have a free account on both sites with an up-to-date profile. If this is totally new to you then both sites provide plenty of help to get you started.

What you are looking to do is to find your contacts and send a connection request through the system. Both have a search facility and it's as simple as typing in their name. Once you have your profile completed then start working through your prioritised list and sending requests to connect.

I recommend you send a personal message when you make a connection request rather than go with the default message. This is useful for people you do not know that well or it has been many years since you last spoke. Sending them a personal message will increase the chances of them being happy to reconnect. You may need to remind them how you know them just in case they have forgotten about you. For family and people you consider as friends then search for them on Facebook and send them a friend request. Also search for them on LinkedIn too as there are some useful features there in terms of giving and receiving connections.

If you cannot find a contact on LinkedIn or Facebook then you can always try typing their name into the Google search engine. You may find a website for them or a profile on another social networking site like Ecademy.com.

The objective of reconnecting is to start an email conversation that should lead to you either meeting or speaking on the phone. If they have accepted your connection request then take that as a good sign that they are happy to talk. Both Facebook and LinkedIn allow you to send personal messages to people you are connected to on their system without needing to know their email address. Send a message suggesting that you talk on the phone or arrange to meet to catch up. Your emphasis should be on catching up with what *they* are doing rather than what you are doing.

Asking Your Contacts For Help

If you want to get the maximum benefit from your existing network in terms of sales-lead generation then it really pays to make it easy for people to help you. One essential way to make it easy for people to help you is by having a clear proposition statement and example stories to be able to illustrate the type of person you want to meet and why they would want to meet you. You will be using these as part of the conversation when you meet or speak on the telephone.

Additionally you make it easy for people to help you by asking for things that would be easy for them to do and have minimal risk or inconvenience to them. If your contact has experience of your work and they know you, like you, and trust you then making a referral will probably not be a big personal risk to them. For others there are ways in which they can help you that are less risky. I always find that seeing things from the other person's perspective helps me to assess what would be reasonable to ask for.

For the remainder of the chapter we will be looking at various help you could ask for from your network that would help you generate more sales-leads. I have provided a range of asks, some of which are easy from people you do not know very well to others that will probably need a good relationship and healthy emotional bank account.

Asking For Referrals

I meet many people who are well aware of the power of referrals. They have a large, trusted network who want to help them. The only trouble is that their proposition has been too vague or generalised for their links to understand how they could refer business to them.

If you have people on your list where this is true, arrange to meet up or have a telephone conversation for an update on what you are each currently doing. You should not just be seeking direct referrals into clients but also for everything we will be covering in this chapter.

If you set up the meeting correctly then you can avoid any awkwardness in asking for referrals. Say at the beginning of the meeting something like:

"It's great to catch up with you after all this time. Can I make a suggestion? Let's update each other with what we are currently doing and then see how we can help each other with introductions and referrals. Is that OK with you?" Then make sure you always focus on the other person before asking for yourself.

Ask For Connections To Competitors

This is not as crazy as it sounds and it is something that can be quite easily asked for where the relationship is relatively new. Most of my early clients came from referrals from competitors and they still do from time to time. If you properly differentiate yourself from your competitors then it becomes much easier. Maybe they specialise in working with large clients and you only work with small ones. Maybe they focus on the North and you focus on the South or maybe you just do something that does not fit their profile.

 As long as your competitors do not see you as a threat then they could become a good potential source of leads. Clearly not everyone will be open to a discussion but some will and an introduction from your existing links could make the process go a lot smoother. You may find that your competitors will charge you a finder's fee if you win the business and you should think of this as a sales and marketing cost.

One of the areas I focused on in the early days of my business was NLP training. I was passed several really good projects from sales training companies who did not have any expertise in NLP. One of these turned out to be a significant NLP modelling project working with a large sales team. The finder's fee I paid was a lot more than the competitor normally earned in a year from an average client at that time. They would not have won business with this particular client and so it turned out a win for all involved, including the client. I helped them discover what their top performing sales people were doing differently to their average sales people and helped them set up their own internal sales training department.

If you provide services then a competitor may also consider using you as an associate which means you work with the client under their brand rather than direct. This can be a good source of cash flow and example stories early in your business and definitely worth considering, especially in the early years of business when you are looking to get established.

Ask For Connections To Potential Alliances

With alliances you are looking for people who are already doing business with the people you want to do business with. The two businesses will have complementary products or services and together form a stronger proposition. Alliances can be a short cut for a younger business to grow quickly and they are great for more established businesses too.

Examples of alliances between major brands include Costa Coffee and high street book stores like Waterstones. I was recently on a short holiday in Bath, England, and as I walked down one particular street I noticed two book stores in the same street, both with a major brand coffee shop located within the store. They had obviously seen the benefit of the coffee shop attracting people into the book store and people going to buy a book who would like a cup of coffee.

Alliances can work for any size of organisation and especially for the relatively new business. Alliances that I have seen working successfully for smaller businesses have included:

- Sales consultant and contact management software vendor
- Web designer and PR consultant
- IT consultant and provider of a remote backup service
- Book writing coach and a publisher
- Management trainer and sales trainer

In thinking through what type of business would make a good alliance you need to think about who is already doing business with the people you want to reach and how your product or service could complement theirs.

Once you have a clear idea as to what type of organisations would make a good alliance, ask your contacts for introductions to people they know in such organisations. Having a personal introduction will normally be much quicker than just making direct contact. I know people who have cold called a potential alliance and gotten totally ignored only to get a quick meeting following an email introduction from a mutual contact.

Ask For Help With PR Opportunities

An important aspect of getting the word out about your products and services is through Public Relations (PR). Traditionally this has been the offline media such as newspapers, journals, radio, and TV. Through my network I have had lots of PR opportunities passed to me. I have been on local radio a few times and have had articles published in business related journals as a result of help from people in my network. I have yet to appear on TV but have been put forward a couple of times for reality TV programmes. I even have people in my network who edit business journals with good circulations and have published my articles from time to time.

Asking your contacts for introductions to editors and journalists in relevant publications is another way people in your network may be able to help you.

These days PR is as much online as it is offline. There are all sorts of opportunities online to get noticed. Here are a couple:

BLOGS/ARTICLES

Blogs are like short articles. You can write your own blog and you can use your network to help publicise it to their network. Twitter is a very easy way for people to do this. Sites like Ecademy.com allow people to post a blog and then have them publicised via Twitter. They can also send them out in their newsletter. Writing a guest blog for a site with high traffic will certainly get you noticed. You can use your network to help you achieve this type of opportunity. There are special sites for articles and you can often submit your articles to these sites for free or low cost. People who are looking for good content for their newsletters and websites go there to look. Journalists for offline media also go to these sites looking for experts.

SOCIAL MEDIA

This includes sites such as LinkedIn, Facebook, and Ecademy. You have the ability to post on forums and answer questions in your area of expertise. I find that people who like what you post online may be motivated to meet you offline.

Questions and answers are very popular, especially with LinkedIn. You could ask one of your contacts to post a question that you want to answer. You will have to allow for others to answer too but you have the opportunity to be the most visible answer.

Asking For Help With Seminars

Seminars and workshops can be very good for starting off a trusted relationship, especially if you are selling services and expertise. They can be an excellent vehicle to raising your profile and getting the word out. Seminars are also a great vehicle for generating sales-leads by including example stories in them.

For example: I worked with a consultant who was really frustrated as to why he was not generating any leads from his seminars. People said they found them interesting but no one was buying. When I went through them with him it was obvious that he was focusing too much on the technology rather than how the technology can make a difference to the audience. We developed some example stories to help illustrate his seminar. He thought people might think he was doing a sales pitch. The result was quite the opposite. Not only did he generate a significant amount of business from every seminar he subsequently ran but the audience stated on the feedback that they found the stories really useful.

You do not have to run your own seminars. You can ask your network for people they know who have opportunities for speakers. There are plenty about who run events and are seeking people who can do a good seminar without it being a glorified sales pitch. Sometimes you will get paid but provided the audience is right then it is a good opportunity to generate sales-leads from your target audience and get someone else to worry about getting people along. Seminars can be at events but also can include tele-seminars and webinars which are both becoming increasingly popular. Again, once you begin asking your network then you will find that you start getting more and more opportunities to do seminars.

If you decide to run your own seminars and workshops then you can utilise your network to publicise your event. You could give people in your network a discount voucher as an added incentive.

When I first started running my public Lead Generation Master Class I invited some people in my network along for free and asked that they let people in their network know they were attending and why. It was a huge success. This is a technique I have used many times. I also have asked my network for a connection to a contact of theirs to offer them a free place onto a seminar I know will be of benefit. This was a very easy ask to make from my network and it allowed me to get to know the invitee and at the same time build credibility.

Asking Your Contacts For Advice

Some people find asking family and close friends for help in relation to business very difficult. For some it even extends to clients. If this is the case for you then a very useful technique is to ask for advice.

When you are ready in terms of having your proposition and stories worked out then start to contact these people and arrange to meet them for a coffee and an update. Let them know you are seeking their advice or input. At the meeting spend a while with the normal small talk and catching up with their news. Then talk them through your proposition together with some example stories and then ask them who they think you should be speaking to. Your proposition statement and the stories will help them to think of people they know who might have similar problems.

I know people who have used this advice approach to start reconnecting and have ended up winning business directly from the people they have sought advice from! I believe this worked because they were sincerely asking for advice rather than using it as a ploy. If you do believe that specific contacts need your services then it would be better to contact them and say that you have an idea you would like to 'run past them'. For example, a call might go something like this:

"Hi Jane, last time we were talking you mentioned that you were having a problem with **<the problem>.** I have been thinking about it and wondered if you are open to meeting up to talk through a couple of ideas."

I have used the advice approach many times, especially with clients I do not think need a specific product or service but probably knows someone who does. I have always benefited in some way from the advice given, even if it had been input into further developing the proposition.

Summary

Our existing network provides us with lots of opportunities to ask for help with generating sales-leads and helping us find our ideal clients. We should begin with clients but we should also aim to reconnect with people that we have not been in contact with for a while but all of whom may be able to help us in some way. Facebook and LinkedIn will help you to reconnect with people you have lost touch with. Having clarity over your proposition and example stories will really help when reconnecting as will being sensitive to what is a reasonable level of help to ask for.

nine

MAKING THE MOST
OF YOUR SALES-LEADS

David had started to get in touch with people in his network. He particularly liked the idea of going back to people he already knew and asking for their advice. He was quickly starting to get some traction and generating enquiries about his services.

He came back to me saying that the sales-leads had started coming in but nothing was resulting from them. Whilst this was a major step forward David recognised that he had to start closing some sales.

"It's so frustrating!" David sighed "When I first start talking to them they are all excited and cannot wait to meet me. Once I put in a proposal it's as if they have disappeared without a trace!"

Introduction

The majority of this book has so far focused on how to generate more sales-leads through your existing network. This is because, in my opinion, generating sufficient quality sales-leads is a big problem in sales, especially with people within small and medium sized businesses that do not have the marketing budgets of some of the bigger organisations.

Sales leads which have been generated through networking, especially referrals, normally make business much easier to win, but I do come across a lot of people that are good at generating lots of interest in what they do yet struggle to turn the initial interest into a sale.

In this chapter we will be looking at how to recognise a sales-lead and then what to do with it to maximise your chances of winning the sale.

The Sales Sausage Machine

When I was new to sales it took a while for me to get the whole thing into perspective. My mentor at the time encouraged me to think of sales in terms of a sausage machine. You know, one of those old fashioned cast iron things with a long body, a hopper on the top and a big handle on the side. You put the sausage meat in the hopper, turn the handle, and the sausages come out the other end. As the sausage meat moves through the machine it is transformed from raw sausage meat into juicy sausages. Although some of it gets wasted, if you put enough good quality sausage meat in the hopper and turn the handle you will get plenty of good quality sausages. You can even start to predict how many sausages you will make each month.

The sausage meat, in sales terms is the sales-leads and the sausages are the sales. The barrel is the process for transforming a sales-lead into a quality sale and the handle is the activity that is required to move the sales-lead through the process. In sausage machine terms it is easy to understand that unless you put sausage meat into the machine you will not get any sausages out the other end. If you put the sausage meat in but there is no transformation process then no sausages will get made. Also the process could be fine but if nobody turns the handle then, again, no sausages.

In order to get consistent sales you need to consistently generate sales-leads and then convert them into sales. Not every sales-lead will successfully become a sale so you need enough sales-leads to allow for those that do not go anywhere. We need to understand that a sales-lead is an expression of interest that needs further work in terms of turning the interest into a real sales opportunity and then converting the sales opportunity into a sale. People fairly new to sales often may miss the signs of an expression of interest and let a sales-lead pass them by.

Recognising Expressions Of Interest

Sometimes a prospect will express quite clearly that they are interested in finding out more about your product or service. It will normally come in the form of a question such as:

- Asking the price
- Asking about a detail such as colour or timing
- Asking for more information

When someone takes an interest in a product or service it does not guarantee that they have any intention of buying but it does suggest that they are in 'buying mode'.

These slight changes in a prospect's behaviour are often called buying signals and you should use these signals to alert you that you have a raw sales-lead. If your prospect specifically asks you something to do with pricing or you can spot them doing something like checking prices then it is a pretty clear signal that there is some interest there but it does not mean they want to buy. It just means you need to go through a process of finding out what is on their mind to see if you have a sales opportunity or not.

When listening to your example stories people could ask questions like:

"How did you do that?" or "What did that involve?" or "That sounds just like me!" People could also give away interest through their actions or body language. For example, they may spend more time looking at one particular item than another or their voice tone or posture change when listening to one of your example stories.

If you notice a buying signal then your first action should be to acknowledge it in some way and use it to stimulate a conversation that will either confirm your suspicions or reveal what's really on their mind. Launching into a sales pitch before knowing what they are seeking to buy is not an effective approach to selling.

I think of it in terms of lighting a fire. We have a spark of interest and to get that spark to take hold we need to put on some kindling to catch light. Once the kindling has caught alight and is starting to burn we have the raw materials for a fire. We need to fan the flames and put on some twigs and small pieces of wood. When they catch light then we can start burning the more substantial material. In sales terms, the equivalent of a sales-lead is the point at which the kindling starts to catch light. You do not have a sale, just an expression of interest. It is your job to turn that spark of interest into a roaring fire. Fortunately there is a simple process for doing just that.

The Process Of Selling

I have found that one of the differences between sales amateurs and professionals is that sales professionals follow a consistent process for turning interest into a sale and they are always working on fine tuning that process. There is no perfect universal sales process. Each business may do things slightly different and it is important for you to develop your own process. Sales processes do tend to go through similar stages and what I am going to do here is present you with a place to start.

The stages of this process are as follows:

1. Generate Interest
2. Qualify Interest
3. Discover problem
4. Propose solution
5. Negotiate sale
6. Agree sale
7. Deliver on your promises

A sale will always go through each stage of your sales process, just as water coming into your home will go through every inch of the water pipes that carry it into your home. Just as with water, some of your sales opportunities may "leak out" along the way. We may want to let some of our sales-leads leak out if they prove unattractive. There are appropriate activities to be done at each stage to move it onto the next stage. Failing to do such activities can significantly affect whether or not a sales-lead turns into a sale.

1. GENERATE INTEREST

The majority of the book up to this point has been about generating interest. How that interest normally manifests for you needs to be determined. The obvious ones are telephone or email based enquiries or referrals. It could happen when you are meeting up with someone for a one-on-one meeting or even at a networking event. When you get an expression of interest then it should be qualified to check whether it really is a sales opportunity.

2. QUALIFY INTEREST

The purpose of this sales stage is to see whether or not there is genuine interest. Many people who do not have enough business will try and sell to everyone. I want you to realise that this approach is wrong as it diminishes your most valuable resource: time. I have also seen others who have not followed up on sales-leads because they assumed they were a waste of time only to see a competitor land a big sale from the so-called 'time waster'. Hopefully by now you have a much clearer understanding of your target audience and what drives their buying motivation.

Every expression of interest should go through this stage and by the end of the qualification process you will have made a conscious decision whether or not there is a real sales opportunity and confirm that you are committed to pursue it all the way to the end of the sales process. The reality is that once you start to go down the sales process you need to continually ask yourself "Are we wasting each other's time?" In that sense we need to continually qualify out opportunities. The initial qualification involves answering for ourselves the following minimum questions:

- How did they come to hear about you?
- What motivated the prospect to express an interest?
- Which Customer Archetype are they?
- Does the prospect have a problem you can solve for them?
- What have they done about the problem so far?
- Who will be involved in making the final decision?
- How easy will it be to get to the decision makers?
- What kind of ball-park budget have they set aside?
- What kind of time scale are they looking at?

Please note that these are not the specific questions you will ask to discover the information. This is quite a lot of information and you may need to set aside time to have a discussion. One of the most important things to find out straight away is what motivated them to express an interest in the first place. This will not only provide you with important information about what they are looking to do but also give you clues as to which Customer Archetype group they belong to. You would say something like:

"Thank you for the enquiry, I know this is going to sound like a silly question, but what motivated you to contact me today?"

In the chapter on Customer Archetypes I included an example of how a client had chosen to respond differently to enquiries from each Customer Archetype. The motivation question is what helped staff to categorise the enquiry.

Asking the motivation question is especially important for a price enquiry. It will tell you what is on their mind and provide enough information to respond appropriately.

When asking for budget I rarely expect them to reveal the exact amount. I get around this by seeking a ball park figure.

For example...

> **Me:** What kind of budget have you set aside for this project?
>
> **Prospect:** We do not have a budget yet
>
> **Me:** That's not a problem. Our clients normally budget anywhere from £1,000 to £100,000 – is that going to be an issue for you?

This approach will ensure their expectations fall within your acceptable range and help eliminate anyone whose expectations are below your required level.

3. DISCOVER THE PROBLEM

Once you are satisfied that you are working with someone who is open to having a sales conversation, then the next stage is to discover the facts that will enable you to propose a solution. The way I learnt to think about this stage is to imagine you are a doctor and the prospect is the patient coming to you for a cure to their ailment. A doctor will ask questions and perhaps do some tests before making a diagnosis and writing a prescription. Your prescription will be the sales proposal. The great thing is that if you ask the right questions and listen carefully to the answers, your prospect will tell you exactly how to propose your solution in a way that will be irresistible to them.

It is possible at this stage of the sales process to identify that you cannot help your prospect. If this is the case then you should let the prospect know and bring the sales process to a close. There is no point wasting your time working on a proposed solution unless there is a fighting chance you will win the deal. Many prospects may just ask you for a proposal as a way of ending the discussion. Much better to spend the time on generating new sales-leads rather than wasting time pursuing a sales opportunity you stand little chance of winning.

Many people see this stage in terms of a meeting but it's much more than that. During this stage you will be asking lots of open questions in order to gather the information you require. You may need to speak to people other than the decision makers in order to get the complete picture.

For example, with one particular client I was talking to them about a sales management coaching programme. I met the Chief Executive and as a result of the meeting agreed to meet with three of his Sales Managers in order to get their input before creating my sales proposal. At that meeting we identified certain issues which radically changed the nature of my proposal.

You also need to aim to speak to anyone who will have an influence in the final decision. This is to extract as much information as possible about what their idea of the solution is and to seek to get their support for your being part of the solution.

4. PROPOSE SOLUTION

This stage is where the real selling begins. You know what the prospect wants and needs, you understand the buying motivation, the expectations in terms of solution and pricing, and what they need to be able to say "Yes!"

Someone selling television sets in an electrical store may do this verbally. They have asked their prospect details about what they are looking for, price, size etc in the previous sales stage. At this point they may say something like:

"Well, given your requirements the television sets I recommend are these ones", and then point them out. The assistant has presented their proposed solution and it's as simple as that.

More complex sales may require a proposal or even a formal sales presentation but each are just ways of presenting your sales proposal. Let's be clear. At this stage of the sales process you are presenting to win! You need to pull out all the stops and make sure that you are presenting your solution in the best possible light.

I was asked by a coaching client why they thought a prospect had gone silent after such a great meeting and giving a verbal agreement. When I saw her "proposal I was shocked (and I am not easily shocked!). She had put forward a proposal for a

£100,000 project via an email. The email was long and rambling and focused on how great her services are rather than why they should agree to her proposal.

A proposal is a selling document. This lady's email would probably be compared against proposals from other potential suppliers. I would hope that some of her competitors did a professional looking document and presented a compelling sales case. Her prospect would probably need to consult other people in the company for that kind of expenditure. The proposal needs to be capable of selling for you to those you may not get to meet – like the Finance Director. This lady's proposal just made her look like an amateur.

The sales proposal should contain the essence of the information extracted from your discovery stage combined with your solution. Whether it is written or presented it will essentially contain the following information in this order:

1. Background to the proposal
2. Current situation
3. Desired Outcome
4. Your Proposed solution
5. Specific benefits of the solution
6. Costs
7. Why they should choose you
8. Credibility / references
9. Terms and conditions

Notice that costs are way down the list. When someone asks you for the price or rates you need to side step the issue and take them through the sales process so that they are able to see the costs in the context of the sales proposal. To do otherwise means that they will not have any context to consider the price compared to alternatives - including doing nothing.

5. NEGOTIATE THE SALE

Once you have proposed your solution then you go through a process of talking through their response to your proposed solution. They may come back with questions or things they want to change. Alternatively there could be issues with things like timing or costs. This is often called "Overcoming objections" but I like to think of it as negotiating towards a win-win sale.

Occasionally, like in David's case, a prospect will give you their undivided attention and even be hurrying you up only to disappear off the planet once you have delivered your proposal. This could be for many reasons and it is sometimes called the "slow no" by sales professionals. You can reduce the number of times this happens by finding out the prospect's process at the discovery stage. You can inoculate against the 'slow no' by setting an agreement that you will discuss the proposal and make the necessary changes. You should also make it clear that you would rather be told no if they are not interested. Some people are "too nice" to say no and if you make it OK then they will be straight with you and prevent you wasting your time.

The negotiation stage is about so much more than discussing price. My first assumption is that if there is an issue with the cost then you need to negotiate the contents of the solution rather than reduce the prices of individual components. Going back to our television set sales assistant, he may offer them alternative cheaper television sets or maybe even a discount if they buy another product at the same time.

My aim here is to give you the essence of this stage of the sales process. Negotiation and objection handling is a big subject and there are lots of great books that give excellent advice.

6. AGREE THE SALE

This is the final stage of the sale and it is about getting a final decision. In highly competitive situations you may need to get training on advanced closing skills. If you have followed the advice of this book then you should find that your competition is significantly reduced and this part of the sale is a formality.

7. DELIVER ON YOUR PROMISES

If you want to create a client who comes back again and again, pays their bill, and gives referrals then it goes without saying that you need to deliver on the agreed solution. This is where all great example stories will come from, together with opportunities for referrals and follow-on sales.

Summary

Generating a consistent flow of sales-leads is essential to producing a dependable sales income. It is also essential to make the most of your sales-leads by developing and consistently following a sales process that converts a sales-lead into a sales opportunity and then onto a won sale. A good sales process will allow you to distinguish the genuine sales opportunities from those that will be a waste of time.

ten

FITTING IT ALL IN

Six months later I got a call from David inviting me to meet up for coffee. David had been incredibly busy delivering on business he had recently won by leveraging his network. In fact he had been so busy in delivering the consulting work to clients that he had been unable to keep in touch with his network. As a consequence the sales-leads had started to dry up. He realised he was in the classic "feast or famine" syndrome. The money was great while it lasted but now he was back to famine.

"However do people find the time to network when they are really busy?" David asked me.

Introduction

Finding time to consistently generate sales-leads can be a real challenge, especially for people who are selling their own services and have to fit sales activity around the delivery of their services. A common reason people do not take the time to network is the perception that there is not enough time to do so. Yet as we have seen with David, the lack of consistent sales-lead generation is behind the classic feast or famine syndrome.

In this chapter we look at ways to be more effective with your time when networking and to be able to keep your network active especially during busy times.

Be A Conversation Starter

You do not have to go to networking meetings to start making connections. People are everywhere. There are people at your health club, people at your speaking club, people on the aeroplane, people at your client's site. If you take an interest in other people and want to expand your network then you do not need to go far. You just need to be prepared to smile and say "Hello".

Start off by making small talk. The weather is always a safe option in the UK. When I talk to people at my health club I simply ask them if they are a hotel guest or a club member. I rarely find anyone who is not happy to have a conversation. Sometimes we end up asking what each other does for a living but other times it is just an enjoyable conversation.

Getting used to starting conversations with random people in my health club gave me the confidence to start off conversations with people at places like exhibitions and on aeroplanes. I find most people are more than happy to talk but are reluctant to be the first one to break the ice and start the conversation. Be the one to take the initiative and you will find you make a lot more connections. When it does come to explaining what you do then make sure you use your proposition statement and example stories. I have generated many quality sales-leads as a result of chance meetings with people who responded to a story.

Use Your Network To Quickly Grow Your Network

In a previous chapter we looked at leveraging your network to generate sales-leads by tapping into their links. You can also tap into those links to quickly grow a quality network. If you do not think that you are very well connected then find some people who are. You will find that they are typically easy to get on with if they can see you are interested in helping them rather than just yourself. It may take you a while to develop a trusted relationship with these people but what you are looking for is for them to introduce you to well connected people they know. When they make the introduction then the relationship with the new connection will probably happen much faster and they may be more willing to help you.

The value of such a network is in the quality of the links. The more well-connected people you add into your network the better connected you can become. You can quickly build a quality network of your own without having to attend any networking group. The network will only be of any use if you are investing some time and value into the network. It is that personal investment which keeps it alive. Remember the emotional bank account? If you only ever seek withdrawals without making deposits your network will quickly suffocate and die. The best time to make deposits into your network is when you do not need anything so that you earn the right to ask when you do need something.

Things that can help swell your emotional bank account could be providing them with connections you think might be useful. It could, however, be acting as a sounding board and providing advice and guidance. It could be as simple as providing uplifting banter whenever you meet. These relationships will never last unless both people like and enjoy the company of the other.

Combine Networking With Meal Times

We have looked at quickly expanding your network of well connected people without ever needing to attend any networking meetings. It still takes time meeting these new contacts and one way to fit in networking when very busy is to combine it with meal times. Whether breakfast, lunch, or dinner there is an opportunity to meet up and eat at the same time. There is something about networking over food that helps foster better relationships.

Join A Networking Group

Many of the organised networking groups involve meeting at meal times. One of the benefits of joining a group is that you get to build trust with people over time. People you meet at such events could become customers but more importantly they can become introducers and provide you with a quality local network. When you have been networking for a while these meetings are even more valuable for keeping in touch with people you already know, rather than making new contacts.

Making time for these networking groups can be very time effective as the real value is in nurturing many relationships in a very time effective manner. If you have a group of thirty people who meet regularly then you are able to keep in touch with thirty people all in one go.

There are many possibilities to network and I am going to name a few of my favourites. They are mostly based in the UK but there may be well equivalent groups in your area.

BREAKFAST

In the UK there are many networking groups that meet at breakfast which seem to be a very popular time to meet.

BNI have meetings all over the country and you attend each week. The networking is structured towards getting to know other people in the group and passing each other referrals. It is "closed", in that each meeting will not allow competing with one-another. BNI is an international organisation available in many countries, all with an identical winning format.

4Networking is open networking in that you can have multiple people from the same profession and also there is less structure - although there is enough for people who find networking a little daunting. One of the great things about 4Networking is that you actually have time in the meeting for one-on-one conversations. This is something that all networks encourage but in 4Networking they promote the behaviour by making it part of the meeting.

My favourite breakfast meeting is NRG Metropolitan which seems to attract the more sophisticated networker that is used to collaborating and helping each other win business. I attend the London event which is well worth my getting up extra early in the morning and making the two hour journey!

Other good breakfast meetings include the Chambers of Commerce and Institute of Directors. Quite often local firms of accountants and lawyers run their own breakfast networks.

LUNCH TIME

Lunchtime networking seems to be more popular with certain professionals and less popular with others. NRG Networks is one that I particularly like. It actively promotes building advocate networks and there is a nice relaxed structure to their meetings.

I have spoken at several local Athena women's network meetings which also meets at lunchtime; their structure is effective and, again, very relaxed. It does encourage the passing of referrals in a very soft and sophisticated way.

The Institute of Directors and Chambers of Commerce run lunch time events too – normally with much less structure to them.

EVENING

Evening meal events happen too but these tend to be more sandwiches and a drink at the bar in the early evening.

Business Scene run large networking events in the early evening which are supported by many of the breakfast and lunchtime networks.

The Institute of Directors and Chambers of Commerce do run evening events, normally with a speaker. Ecademy events are often done on a similar basis.

Organise Your Own Exclusive Networking Meetings

If organised networking is not of interest or you are too busy to attend or travel a lot, then why not organise your own.

You organise a meal at a restaurant on a specific day and then invite people to join you. This could be breakfast, lunch or dinner. Let everyone know that they will be sharing the bill or paying for themselves. All you need to do is book the table and invite people. I normally go for a maximum of ten people. That keeps it intimate but big enough that I am able to have updates from several people at one time. This is just like a dinner party at home except that we are at a local restaurant.

From time to time I get requests from people in my network who want to meet people I know from larger corporates. They want a meeting but cannot tell me why the other person would want to talk to them. What I have done a few times is organise a dinner for people I know and invite a small group of people including the person who wanted the meeting and the contact he wanted to meet. There are no pitches at my dinners but people do talk to one another about what they do.

Another format I use if I am very busy and want to meet new people is run one of my evening dinners with a twist. I invite five people I know well and ask each one to bring along someone they know well and who is well connected. That expands the network of everyone present but also makes it easy for people to introduce their contacts in an informal way.

You can always restrict your networking meetings to one person and make that at breakfast, lunch or dinner. That is good when you want to get to know each other better. I tend to meet people for a cup of coffee when time allows as the cost of eating out can quickly add up. Being busy with billable work, however, makes it much easier to justify the cost.

Use Online Business Networking

Online sites like Facebook, LinkedIn and Ecademy are extremely effective time saving devices for building your network and staying in touch with your existing network. There are more online social networks being created all the time. Most of the new ones seem to be focused on specific areas of common interest. I find that most people I know either use Facebook and/or LinkedIn in addition to the specialist online social networks. The specialist networks like Ecademy are good for making new connections but I normally end up keeping in touch with them on LinkedIn or Facebook once I get to know them.

Look After Your Advocates

I always say that one good advocate is worth ten clients. When I go networking I am normally looking for potential advocates rather than clients. What gets exciting about having a network of advocates is that provided you look after your direct advocates then your reputation will start to grow through their networks.

I am regularly amazed at how badly some people treat their advocates. I had one company who I had been advocating and had referred to them almost £50,000 of business over a couple of months. When I decided to use them for my own business they took advantage of the relationship and gave me a very sloppy service saying they were too busy with other clients. The clients I had referred to them by the way! I did not recommend them again and actually gave my revised feedback of their service to several people who were interested in using their services. Because my needs were miniscule compared to the clients I referred I was given a second-class service. The service they gave me could also be given to someone I advocate so I could no longer recommend them.

Many of my best advocates have never paid me a penny for the help I have given them. They are not in my ideal audience and yet they are in a great position to recommend me to their clients. Always expect a good advocate to want to check you out in some way. Maybe they will want to sample your services. Another option is to introduce them to your clients who hopefully will be happy to advocate you. When selling IT I used to judge the quality of a client relationship based on whether a client would be prepared to share the stage with me at a public seminar. I am pleased to report that many did!

Happy Networking!

I hope you have found the contents of the book useful and are beginning to think about networking in new ways. I hope that you:

1. Have a clear proposition statement that emphasises your area of specialization and the value you add to your clients in fifteen words or less.
2. I hope you now have some compelling example stories that are memorable and illustrate your proposition statement.
3. I hope you are now starting to think about how you can build and leverage your network in the most effective manner.
4. I hope you are beginning to think about your process for converting sales-leads into new business; and
5. I hope you are networking in a time effective and sustainable way so that you can maintain your network when you are busy

And if you are doing all of that properly and with the right mindset then you will generate more quality sales-leads from your networking and have a lot of fun in the process.

ABOUT THE AUTHOR

Richard White is a sales coach and trainer for small and medium sized technology companies. He specialises in enabling clients to win more business from large companies through effective networking. Richard is a sought after speaker on the subject areas of business networking and sales communication.

Richard holds an MBA from Cranfield School of Management where he specialised in the marketing of services. He worked as a business intelligence consultant for over 10 years working for Oracle before going on to build a successful consulting practice for an Oracle partner.

Richard is a Master NLP Coach and Master NLP Practitioner and is skilled in helping technically minded people feel more comfortable about sales. He is known as The Accidental Salesman® and is the founder of TheAccidentalSalesman.com.

Richard is a recent convert to trekking having fulfilled a lifetime ambition of visiting Machu Pichu in Peru. He is also a regular visitor to the cinema and enjoys dinner parties with friends.

You can contact Richard at rwhite@theaccidentalsalesman.com

RESOURCES

There are hundreds of free articles, audios, videos, and e-books on networking and other sales and marketing related topics for accidental sales people at *www.theaccidentalsalesman.com*

Like other thought leaders, I stand on the shoulders of giants. Over the last twenty years I have attended countless trainings and read hundreds of books which have all impacted my philosophy in some way. Below I list some of the books that have made a significant impact on my thinking in relation to the topics covered in this book.

Networking

The World's Best Known Marketing Secret by Ivan R. Misner PhD, Virginia Devine, Bard Press, 1999

Masters of Networking by Ivan R. Misner PhD and Don Morgan MA, Bard Press, 2000

Seven Second Marketing by Ivan R. Misner PhD, Bard Press, 1996

Business by Referral by Ivan R. Misner PhD & Robert Davis, Bard Press, 1998

Networking for Life by Thomas Power, Ecademy Press, 2003

And Death Came Third by Andy Lopata and Peter Roper, www.Bookshaker.com, 2006

Relationships

How to Win Friends and Influence People by Dale Carnegie, Simon & Schuster, 1981

How to Have Confidence and Power in Dealing With People by Les Giblin, Prentice Hall, 1956

Making Friends by Andrew Matthews, Media Masters, 1990

Communication

Made to Stick by Dan and Chip Heath, Arrow Books, 2008

NLP at Work by Sue Knight, Nicholas Brealey Publishing, 1992

Never be Boring Again by Doug Stevenson, Cornelia Press, 2003

Unleashing the Ideas Virus by Seth Godin, Simon & Schuster, 2002

All Marketers are Liars by Seth Godin, Penguin Books, 2007

The Tipping Point by Malcolm Gladwell, Abacus, 2001

Sleight of Mouth by Robert Dilts, Meta Publications, 1999

Sales

Sales on a Beermat by Mike Southon and Chris West, Random House, 2005

Non-manipulative Selling by Dr Tony Alessandra, Fireside, 1992

Diary of a Naked Salesman' by Espen Holm, Elixir Publishing, 2002

Zero-Resistance Selling by Maxwell Malz, Dan Kennedy et al, Prentice Hall, 1998

Relationship Selling by Jim Cathcart, Perigee, 1990

The Psychology of Selling by Brian Tracy (Audio CD), Nightingale Conant, 1995

Successful Selling with NLP by Joseph O'Connor and Robin Prior, Thorsons, 2000

Other

The Acorn Principle by Jim Cathcart, St Martin's Press, 1998

The 7 Habits of Highly Effective People by Stephen R. Covey, Simon & Schuster, 1992

The Beermat Entrepreneur by Mike Southon and Chris West, Prentice Hall, 2002

Six Thinking Hats by Edward de Bono, Bay Back Books, 1999

The Gorillas Want Bananas by Debbie Jenkins and Joe Gregory, Lean Marketing Press, 2003

Awaken the Giant Within by Anthony Robbins, Pocket Books, 1992

Unlimited Power by Anthony Robbins, Simon & Schuster, 1989

Predictably Irrational by Dan Ariely, HarperCollins, 2008

ALSO FROM BOOKSHAKER.COM

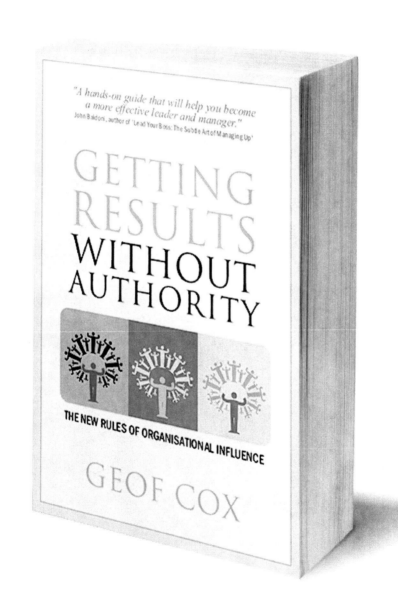

"Beginners and experts alike will find this book filled with useful information. I wish I had had a book like this when I was learning NLP."

Romilla Ready, Lead Author,
NLP for Dummies® & NLP Workbook for Dummies®

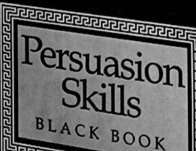

Persuasion Skills
BLACK BOOK

Practical NLP Language Patterns for Getting The Response You Want

Rintu Basu

FREE INSIDE
Black Book
Persuasion
Training
E-course